GIFT OF LOVE

GIFT OF LOVE

KRIS MACKAY

BOOKCRAFT
Salt Lake City, Utah

Library of Congress Catalog Card Number: 90-62187

ISBN 0-88494-756-4

First Printing, 1990

Printed in the United States of America

Contents

Contents

1

Gift of Love

It was one of the most unusual military funerals ever held.

Two rows of top navy brass in crisp full-dress uniform sat at attention in the LDS chapel on Christmas Eve, 1985, saying good-by—with full military honors—to their friend and colleague "Captain" David Karl Clayson.

But Captain Clayson was only eleven years old.

I never met David in person, but I feel as if I know him well. His handsome young face smiles out from the photograph propped against my computer, and something about his eyes convinces me that had I known him we would have been friends. But I understand that's the effect he had on everybody.

Since that Christmas Eve I've visited in his home many times and handled items that were precious to David. I've listened, spellbound, as friends of all ages have told me of his many talents and unusual charisma. Strange how close one may become to a person one has never seen face to face.

And that closeness-by-proxy was the thought that filled the mind of his mother, Jane Stratford Clayson, when she learned that her son had a serious, probably fatal, disease. She sensed that her little boy was frightened, of course, at the prospect of slipping alone into the darkness of the unknown.

If only there were *some way* to introduce him to her late father, to the grandfather he'd never had a chance to meet, the remarkable man who'd died before David was born. If only she could *somehow* bring him close to the loving, compassionate man her father had been when he was alive. It comforted Jane to picture her dad waiting eagerly to welcome her son. If only David could love and trust him as she did, might that not ease the little boy's fear?

So she placed Lt. Comm. Stratford's picture in formal navy choker whites on the table by David's bed, and spent hours telling him stories of his grandfather's heroic accomplishments.

But in her heart she knew that a picture and stories were not enough.

It was February 24, 1945, at the site of some of the bloodiest battles fought in all of World War II. Iwo Jima, 660 nautical miles from Tokyo, was crucial to the United States war effort, and it had to be taken.

Army Air Force planes blasted Iwo for seventy-two days prior to the navy's three-day bombardment. It was a terrible battle. An average of ten American ships per day were blown up by mines or hit by suicide planes. On the island itself the fire was equally deadly. In some units casualties ranged from 20 to 100 percent within the space of hours.

Lt. Comm. E. Wayne Stratford of Portland, Oregon, was Senior Medical Officer aboard the U.S.S. Lubbock (APA 197 attack troop transport). He worked feverishly to save the lives of half-dead men carried back on board with what he termed "garbage can wounds."

Then Dr. Stratford received an order so bizarre that he had difficulty in believing it could be true. For the first time in American military history, medical officers were ordered to designate wounded men who could return to the fight.

Scuttlebutt reached the wounded over the navy's grapevine, and when the unhappy doctor stepped reluctantly into the wardroom he was spared the agony of having to make a choice. Every marine who could struggle off his bed was lined up, in uniform, waiting for Dr. Stratford, volunteering to go back. One lieutenant colonel with five bullet wounds in his back pleaded for permission to return with his men.

Out of 500 patients on the Lubbock, 50 were patched up sufficiently to fight again, plus 32 who weren't up to doing battle but could handle supplies. They joined 3500 wounded from other navy APAs. These heroic volunteers were dubbed the Bandaged Brigade, and from their numbers came the five who were photographed raising the historic flag on Mount Suribachi.

These were desperate times, but men aboard Dr. Stratford's transport were luckier than most. The Lubbock was the first floating penicillin laboratory in the world. At that stage penicillin, barely known, was used only intravenously and was reserved for the most severe cases.

Dr. Stratford devised a method for growing the yeast in bottles. He originated the process of inoculating sterile bandages with the medication, ready for instant application to open wounds. His concept was later picked up and used by the entire navy, and he was honored with a citation from President Franklin D. Roosevelt for the countless lives he'd helped to save.

The navy—and all of America—owed Dr. Stratford an enormous debt of gratitude.

David's problem surfaced out of nowhere just before Christmas 1984. Dr. Karl R. Clayson, noted vascular surgeon, stood in the hospital emergency room holding his son's X-rays in his hand. He was stunned. The pictures highlighted a massive growth on David's brainstem, and

Dr. Clayson's training forced him to acknowledge that it was only a matter of time before David would be gone.

The family—parents Karl and Jane, sisters Janie, seventeen, and Hannah, eleven—were thrust into a state of shock at the prognosis. David was an unusually active, healthy, ten-year-old boy who played baseball and soccer, excelled in every aspect of schoolwork, played the violin almost professionally, and sang in a local children's chorus. He was never sick! Not until that sudden blinding headache at his violin teacher's the afternoon before.

By morning David's balance was gone. His mother held him up as he attempted an unsteady, lurching course down the hallway.

By June he was wheelchair-bound, partially paralyzed, and he had great difficulty with speech. Eventually all that moved were his eyes—up and down for "yes" and from side to side for "no."

Even his mother had to accept then that the son she adored almost beyond reason was approaching the end of his life. She turned his position every hour of the day and night to avoid bedsores, and she wrestled his heavy wheelchair into their station wagon to give him as many outings as possible. There was nothing within her power she wouldn't give to help her little boy.

Friends visited from school and church and brought presents. Jane hired concert pianists, magicians, and clowns to fill the extra hours and to hone the edge on his still-keen mind.

But the gift she wanted most desperately for David— and the one featured most prominently in her prayers— was to ease his passage by somehow helping him to *know* and to *love* the remarkable man he would soon join in death.

How could she give him that priceless gift of love? She

hat off his head and presented it to the youngster; an aviation bosun's mate pushed his own insignia into the hat.

Two cooks baked a special cake and decorated it with:

To David Clayson
Honorary Member
USS *Carl Vinson*

It was a day of unbelievable compassion by men who had been trained for war, not for demonstrations of love. They didn't suspect that they were repaying a debt the navy had long owed to David's grandfather, and in the process fulfilling a mother's prayers.

From that day on they were all friends and shipmates, and David was "Captain" David Clayson. Dick hung a ship's bell by the Clayson front door, to be sounded when the "captain" entered or left the house. As long as one arm could move, David solemnly saluted when Commander Stoeltzing came to call.

David's bedroom was decorated like a room at sea. Someone commandeered a navy blanket to cover the bed.

As the months passed, the men on the *Vinson* didn't forget the boy. They regularly sent autographed photographs or recruiting posters to remind him of the day their paths had crossed.

David's strength continued to wane, and Commander Stoeltzing promoted an outing closer to home. He contacted Air Force Captain Tom Armstrong at Mather Air Force Base in Sacramento and arranged for David to sit at the controls of a huge navy jet.

Once again the wheels of a mighty organization geared for war ground to a halt while men who admired the spirit of the helpless child in the wheelchair acted in a way that was out of character, and made him a vital part of their lives.

Military men were not alone in their devotion for David. His Primary music teacher arranged with a local theatre for a private showing of the movie *E.T.* She wanted him to absorb the gentle message of E.T.'s longing to go home.

The theatre management invited forty of David's friends to join him and in a surprise gesture furnished free popcorn and soft drinks.

David slipped away on December 21, 1985, and his farewell was held on Christmas Eve. One thousand people gathered to honor his memory. His mother and two sisters played their violins as three-fourths of their usual family quartet, while David's smaller violin rested quietly on a music stand by their side.

It *was* an unusual funeral, but not as sad as it might have been. The youngster had packed a lot of living into his final few months, but, most important, his family's prayers for his peace of mind had been answered.

David had gone confidently to meet the grandfather he already loved.

David—like E.T.—had gone *home.*

2

Errand of Love
PART ONE

How quickly do our loved ones become involved after passing through the veil? Is there a time of quiet inactivity, of reorientation?

Or when the prophet Alma states that "all is as one day with God, and time only is measured unto men" (Alma 40:8), does he mean exactly what he says?

Ida Howard was only thirteen when she met Ryan Saxon. She looked and acted considerably older. She was striking in appearance even then, with thick, naturally curly blond hair framing the sweetness of her face, and a wonderfully lilting, operatic-style singing voice. Her new friend was attracted to her on sight.

Ryan was several years older and a returned missionary. By the time he realized how young Ida was, it was too late; they were already hopelessly in love.

When she turned fifteen, they were eager to marry. Ryan was a responsible young man. He solemnly promised Ida's parents that if they would consent to a wedding, their daughter would finish high school and do all the things she would have done if she hadn't married—he would see to it personally—and he and Ida would put off starting a family until her education was complete.

Marrying at fifteen wasn't as unusual as it sounds. In Ridgeland, South Carolina, twenty-six miles from Savannah, Georgia, girls traditionally married young, so her family did agree.

Life took on a blissful, fairytale-like quality for the Saxons. They followed the outline promised to her parents. Ida finished school, and she was twenty years old before daughter Debbie was born. Now they felt they had it all.

Ryan was a small man physically but he was wiry and athletic, and he ran like a streak of lightning. His trophy cabinet held every track award the county offered, to prove it.

Young in years to preside over the LDS South Georgia District (district president, comparable to stake president), he conscientiously carried out all his Church assignments. Maybe he worked harder to compensate for his youth. The little family traveled a lot of miles to cover the wide expanses of the district, while Ryan preached and Ida sang. Yes, they *were* young in years, but they were a striking, dedicated, and talented pair.

By the time Debbie was almost five, Ida was six months pregnant with their second child. Ryan worked at construction with his father and brothers, and he'd started building their dream house. Close to the Lord and more in love all the time, they made life simple and good, and every day it grew better.

One day Ryan was surprised to receive a strong spiritual impression to limit the hours he devoted to hunting. Men in the South spend considerable time with a rifle in their hands, and Ryan was no exception. He'd grown up hunting. Maybe the Lord thought those hours should be put to Church work, and if so Ryan was willing to comply. Whatever the reason, he was obedient to the prompting, and for six months he didn't hunt at all.

But he missed it. He missed the comradery of the open air with his brothers and friends.

One morning the young couple woke to the pleasant splash of raindrops skittering across the roof and the clean smell of rain-freshened air. They had expected it. Rain had been predicted, and contractors don't work outside in the rain. That left Ryan with an important decision to make.

His brothers and a few friends were planning a hunting trip, and they'd invited him to go along. Ryan had nothing pressing to do that day, no Church work that would suffer, and he was sorely tempted. Besides, he wasn't sure the Lord meant *never*.

Almost always up and out of bed early, on this morning he hesitated, unsure, trying to decide.

"Do you think I should go?" he asked his wife. Ida assured him that the decision was entirely his.

He wasn't in any hurry, so they relaxed in the warmth of their bed, and with her curly head on his shoulder they talked lingeringly about many things. It was a time of special closeness.

Finally Ryan decided to go. He got up, showered, dressed in his tan, baggy hunting shirt and the pants that had hung unused in the closet for so long, put on high-top brogans, and topped his outfit off by donning a bright red cap with a bill.

With special tenderness he kissed his wife good-by, jumped into his white sedan, and sped away. He wouldn't be back until the next morning. The men expected to camp out overnight.

That evening Ida was guest soloist at a dinner meeting of the local Business and Professional Women's Club. She finished her song, graciously accepted their applause, and was enjoying dinner when the telephone rang.

Was the bell more strident than usual? To Ida, it seemed that it was. She was startled. With fork halfway to her mouth, she *knew* by the sick feeling in the pit of her stomach that the call was for her.

An accident! Ryan—shot! She had trouble in processing the words. A fellow hunter had spotted movement behind a clump of trees, a blur, a shadow running too rapidly and silently to be anything but a deer. Without hesitation the man had thrown his rifle to his shoulder, aimed through the sights, and squeezed the trigger.

Only it wasn't an animal. Ryan, hurtling soundlessly toward a deer grazing at the top of the hill, had been shattered by the bullet of a friend. The hunter was in shock. Ryan's brothers were speeding Ryan—and the man who shot him—to the nearest hospital.

Ida wasn't told over the telephone that her husband was already dead, but it wasn't necessary. Somehow she knew that, too.

She raced to the hospital. Once there, she couldn't force herself to enter the room where he lay. She'd never seen a dead body up close before, and in panic, she knew she couldn't bear to touch one, not even—maybe especially not even—her husband's.

Dazed and numb, she managed to drive herself back home. Surely she could pull herself together, could cope with the unbelievable a little better by morning.

But the prospect of staying alone in the bedroom she had so recently and tenderly shared with her husband was much too painful, so she slept in a guest room at the front of the house. I say slept, but she couldn't *sleep*, of course.

Before turning down the covers on the unfamiliar bed, Ida stood in shock at the window. The room was dark and bathed in shadows. Suddenly the whole world seemed devoid of light. Without the emotional strength to switch on a light, she stared out with unseeing eyes at the dark, deserted street.

Wait! Not quite deserted. The outline of something bulky caught her attention, something out of its usual place. What was it? She forced her frozen mind to concentrate.

Apparently some helpful friend had returned Ryan's car, parking it across the street under the branches of a huge old magnolia tree. Ida's eyes were riveted to the car in almost hypnotic fascination. Cold white metal shimmered in the moonlight, and the sheer emptiness of it, standing there alone and still, struck her to the heart with the reality of his loss.

Through all the long hours of the night she tossed and turned on the guest bed—and her grief threatened to be more than she could endure.

At last the night was nearly over. The first faint rays of morning lit up the windowpane, and Ida restlessly turned again in the bed.

Idly, her glance fell on the doorway. She blinked, and her breath caught in her throat.

Ryan was standing on the threshold. He was alive!

He was dressed in the same baggy clothes she had watched him put on before he kissed her and drove away. Everything about him looked perfectly natural, and when he spoke his voice sounded exactly like it always had.

"Ida," he said gently, "I've come to tell you good-by. Don't worry about the baby. The birth will go well and the baby will be fine."

Without stopping or waiting for an answer, he continued: "There's something I want you to do for me. Go to my sister Vivian [the family genealogist] and tell her that someone in Uncle Grady's line still needs her temple work done."

And suddenly, Ryan was simply . . . gone.

Now Ida felt a compulsion to see her husband's body. Could the news of his death have been in error? After all, he had come to her in the doorway, speaking as naturally and as lovingly as ever. And yet he *had* told her good-by.

Now she *wanted* to go to the hospital. She needed to see for herself.

But what her husband had asked of her seemed more urgent than going immediately to him. First of all she must visit Vivian and deliver his message.

Very early, as soon as it was completely light, Ida dressed and hurried to the home of her sister-in-law. To-gether they searched through all the records pertaining to Uncle Grady and his family. They looked for any hint that someone listed in the good-sized stack of books and papers had been overlooked. They looked again, and then again.

One last time they pored over each sheet, but this time Vivian turned the pages over instead of sliding them off to the side. And there on the back of one of the records, all alone at the top of the page, they found the name of a woman—Ida. M. Barfield—whose work had not been done, a daughter to the wife of their great grandfather, A. A. Saxon, Mary Frances's child by a former marriage but raised by him.

Every line on the front of the sheet was filled, and temple endowments already performed. That one lone name had been written on the back—and forgotten.

How quickly *do* our loved ones become involved in new lives after passing through the veil?

In Ryan's case, it appeared that no time at all elapsed before he was once again a worker in his Father's kingdom, performing his double errand of love.

3

Errand of Love
PART TWO

Ida's story poses a second question:

After our loved ones are involved in new lives beyond the veil, and especially after the passage of years, do they become too busy or too engrossed to remain as concerned with us as when they were alive?

Life was hard on Ida after the death of her husband, with one terrible, wrenching tragedy following another.

Ten days after Ryan was killed, and while Ida was still reeling with grief, her beloved father passed away with no warning. Shortly thereafter, her father-in-law also unexpectedly died.

Thus in the span of four traumatic months, she lost all three of the most important men in her life.

Ryan's brief return brought her comfort for a time, but

after the birth of her second daughter, Ryna, Ida was dev-astated by the sensation of being absolutely and totally alone.

A friend sent her a dozen roses to celebrate the birth, but roses were the gift Ryan had given her after Debbie was born, and because she was locked in her unreasoning grief the well-intentioned gesture only emphasized to Ida that her babies' father was irrevocably gone.

Ida sobbed for days and could not be comforted.

Worst of all, the testimony she'd counted on to see her through, the faith that had appeared as unwavering as steel with Ryan's strength to lean on, wasn't powerful enough by itself to sustain her now that she was alone.

Ida was horrified to learn how fully she had operated under her husband's light. With the onslaught of one crushing blow after another her spirit drooped, and for a time she couldn't control the darkness that threatened to engulf her.

Eventually she remarried and happiness returned. For fourteen years Ida enjoyed her role as mother to her own two daughters and to her new husband's young daughter and son. They bore a son together.

But suddenly the marriage turned to disaster, and she was flung headfirst back into coping with life by herself.

Actually, the children—all of them—had been her sal-vation. She had managed pretty well while they were young and needed her day-to-day care. Then they grew up, mar-ried, and established their own homes hundreds of miles away. Now Ida was truly alone. And depressed.

And this time, dangerously suicidal.

Over the years as tragedy followed tragedy she had drifted out of Church activity and into habits she'd never dreamed she could embrace. Her situation was serious, she knew, but by herself she couldn't call up the power needed to check the bleak downward spiral of fear and, ultimately, guilt.

Every day Ida sat alone in her Alameda, California, apartment facing the balcony, drawn hypnotically to the finality of the concrete sidewalk below. She was fascinated with imagining how easy it would be to slip over the edge into oblivion.

With each passing moment the balcony's invitation beckoned her more compellingly.

Ida's daughter Ryna was involved in her own life in Provo, Utah. Her husband attended Brigham Young University, at work on his master's degree, and she had a young baby to care for.

But she missed her mother, and sometimes she felt a little uneasy. She knew her mother wasn't happy. Ryna often wished there was something tangible she could do to help.

One night she had a vivid nightmare. She dreamed that her mother was in mortal danger. She woke to the presence of her father, a presence that pervaded the room as positively as a physical touch.

She'd never seen her father—not in this life, at least—but throughout her life she'd felt close to him, had experienced a sense of his love. Totally convinced that he was with her on this occasion, she rose from her bed and searched the room. She called to him out loud: "Daddy! Where are you?"

Ryan didn't show himself to his daughter's mortal eyes, but in her mind she heard him speak. Her mother was indeed in danger, a danger not only of mortal but of eternal significance. She needed help, and it had to be immediate. Ryna was instructed to write her mother a letter. Her father would supply the words.

Ryna ran to her desk, pulled out a sheet of paper, and stuffed it into the typewriter. Then she typed as fast as her fingers could fly over the keys, while her father dictated every word.

It was a firm letter. Her fingers tapped out details about her mother's condition that Ryna had never suspected, and offered specific measures to effect a change.

Then she typed: "You have got to start over. You have been too long regressing.

"You need to talk to your bishop *now*. You need to get the whole sore business of forgiveness over. The bishop has the authority to tell you what the Lord wants, and when you are forgiven. . . . The bishop will help you in mercy and in love. . . . There is no other way. Do not doubt the word of the Lord."

The letter quotes word for word—verbatim—a long sentence from Ida's patriarchal blessing: "And the Lord has given special charge concerning thee, that thou should have *guidance and assistance* given unto thee to overcome the powers of the adversary."

Ryna added a comment or two of her own: "I've been urgently urged to write you. . . . We have a heritage to think about, and I especially want your grandchildren to know how you overcame your trials."

That powerful letter marked the beginning of Ida's fight to gain control of her destiny. It wasn't easy. She says: "I know what hell is like; I've been there. I'll never *allow* myself to go again."

It took years to accomplish her return in full, but the day she received that letter from Ryna was the day she took the first tentative steps on the road to rebuilding her faith.

Her name is Ida Cluff now, and she is one of my closest friends. Any number of people are there to support her should she need to momentarily lean on someone else's strength. But Ida, herself, has changed. She knows that life is not always easy, so she has built up strength in her own right.

She is convinced that, should the need arise again, she will not falter.

So—after our loved ones become involved beyond the veil, are they too busy to be as concerned about our welfare as they were when they were alive?

Ryan certainly wasn't. Years had passed and Ida was living a life he didn't approve of, but Ryan found a way to let her know that he still cared.

4

On a Wing
and a Prayer

Exercised daily, prayer flexes its muscles and develops into a powerful ally.

Let me tell you there are few things in life—if any—that my friend Marion Mealey is more consistent about than exercising *her* spiritual muscles—talking over her trials and triumphs, all her day's activities, with her Father in Heaven. Like everybody else she has problems, but they are seldom more than she and the Lord can handle together.

Marion is a busy lady. She travels a lot, and wherever she goes she's invariably in a hurry. Her husband says she travels on a wing and a prayer.

But miracles wrought by prayer are not by definition always sober affairs. Occasionally, one seems to hear echoes of a heavenly chuckle.

The little beige Volkswagen bus stopped dead on a particularly deserted stretch of country road between Spokane and

Pasco, Washington. The engine that had hummed along merrily all the miles from Rossland, British Columbia, had simply and suddenly, without so much as a cough, ceased to function.

Marion sat hunched over in the driver's seat, her hands still gripping the wheel. She peered out into the blackness of the night. Hers seemed to be the only car on the road. What should she do?

A glance over her shoulder confirmed that Brian, eight, and Lauri, six, were still sleeping soundly in the back seat. She knew nothing about the inner workings of a car, so opening the Volkswagen's rear deck and poking at those mysterious coils and gadgets wouldn't help. And she certainly couldn't start walking who-knew-how-many miles to civilization—not leaving her two sleeping children behind.

Once again it was time for serious prayer.

When she and Danny had moved from Canada, the two older children had asked to be allowed to finish high school in Rossland. Their parents didn't object, except for the prospect of long drives to cart the children to California for visits and equally lengthy trips to return them to relatives in Canada for school.

This time Janice and Jim had really, *"really"* wanted to see Lawrence Welk perform at the California State Fair on Saturday before starting north on Labor Day weekend.

The problem was that Marion *must* be back in Rancho Cordova for work on Monday morning. Setting out on Saturday meant that she—the lone driver—would sit behind the wheel for twenty-one straight hours, drop the kids off, hop back into the car with no time to rest, then drive like the wind to be home again in time for work.

But she was young and strong, and, like most mothers, she liked to say yes when she could. She had no doubt that she could make it. Danny's knack for mechanics kept their car in good working condition, so in fact the journey *had* gone smoothly all the way up to Rossland, and for half of the distance back.

Until a minute or two before, the car had managed better than its driver. Marion had been having great difficulty in keeping her eyes open. As mile after mile of open farmland flew past her window in one long, continuous blur, she became almost hypnotized. She fought to stay awake. It was one-thirty on a clear, dark night between Sunday and Monday, and she hadn't been to bed since Friday. Maybe this wasn't such a good idea after all.

Conversations with the Lord are second nature for Marion, so as the miles passed and she noticed her weariness increasing she pleaded for stamina. "Please, Father, help us to get home safely. Help me to stay awake. Please don't let me injure my children."

Now there they were, stranded, and Marion could think of absolutely nothing to do about it. She was so tired! If she curled up and shut her eyes for just a minute, maybe she could think more clearly after a nap.

The front seat of a Volkswagen is cramped, but in her exhaustion she fell asleep immediately.

She woke an hour and a half later, totally and surprisingly refreshed. More out of desperation than hope of success, she turned the key in the ignition one more time. To her amazement the engine turned over and sprang to life. She put the car in gear and drove the rest of the way home without difficulty of any kind.

If anyone tried to do so, convincing Marion that a loving Father hadn't stretched out his hand and said "Stop— Rest!—Then I'll help you" wouldn't be easy.

Marion remembered that incident ten years later when the same Volkswagen suddenly began to jerk and cough. The children had grown older and so had the faithful little car, but after dozens of trips to Canada to visit her mother through the years, with Danny's manipulations it still performed beautifully. Almost always.

Except for tonight. Marion and Lauri (now sixteen) were further along on the road than they had been the other time, but several hours of driving still lay ahead of them. To judge by the agonized gasps issuing from the bug's ailing engine, they'd never make it.

Marion is not only a busy lady but she's also practical and self-reliant. Moments when she is totally without personal resource are few and far between. One of those times had occurred ten years before, and she began to suspect that tonight might be another one in the making.

Putt-putting along at a fraction of their regular speed, they limped into the small town of Weed, where a garage sign advertised service facilities for foreign cars. Unfortunately it was after hours, and the mechanic had left for the day.

Marion was frantic. She had promised to be home before 11:00 P.M. Her husband worked nights, and their other car was out of commission. Danny needed her car to get to work. She climbed back behind the wheel and they sputtered on down the road.

Before long it was painfully apparent that the car couldn't continue. Marion coasted into a rest stop.

Lauri waited in the car while her mother stepped into the deserted restroom. She and the Lord were alone when she dropped to her knees in prayer.

Speaking to a trusted friend, the desperate woman outlined her problem. With childlike faith, never wavering, knowing that all things are possible to those who believe, she asked that the car might function properly long enough to get them to Rancho Cordova. Once home, Danny would take care of everything.

She returned to the car, started it up, and wasn't the

least bit surprised when it purred to life and then flew over the remaining miles.

Lauri was stunned for a second, but remembering the relationship Marion had built with their Father over a lifetime, she said only, "For goodness' sake, Mother—what did you do in there?"

They were late getting home. Now that the car functioned perfectly they hurried right along, but the hours of limping and sputtering had eaten up too much time and they were late.

Even before they pulled into the driveway, they spotted Danny pacing back and forth in great frustration. He is dependable almost to a fault, and being late for work constitutes, for him, a fate worse than death. He didn't have a moment to waste on polite conversation.

Did he stop to kiss her hello? Marion doesn't remember that he did. Her usually gentle husband was yanking suitcases out of the trunk and heaving them onto the lawn, obviously irate, muttering, "Why didn't you get an earlier start—you knew I needed the car?" as he leaped into the driver's seat, gunned the engine, and roared back out of the driveway.

Marion ran a few steps after the retreating car and called, "Danny, wait! You'll never make it! I only asked to get us home. I didn't ask for the car to get you to work. I thought you'd fix it!"

As his taillights faded in the distance, Marion sighed and turned to carry their suitcases into the house.

It was morning and Marion was just waking up when she heard Danny's key in the lock. He appeared at the bedroom door with a sheepish grin on his face. Last night's anger was gone.

It seemed the effects of Marion's powerful prayer had run out about a mile and a half down the highway. Without warning, the little car resumed its wheezing and then died irrevocably at the side of the road. Danny had trudged to a phone booth and called a friend to ask for a lift. The car would need replacement parts and considerable work before it moved another inch on its own.

Danny sat on the edge of the bed and took Marion's hand in his. This time he was ready to listen.

Ruefully he queried, "Now, what were you telling me when I drove off to work?"

5

The Boy Who Couldn't Swallow

Shortly before the birth of her fourth child, Pat Beadle had a dream. She thought she was in the delivery room where her son had already been born, but his tiny body lay still and lifeless. He wasn't breathing.

She watched as her husband, Doug, and LDS Dr. Cox carefully laid their hands on the baby's limp little head and, as a last resort, gave him a blessing.

Someone else was in the room—and extremely interested. Pat saw a grown man's spirit standing next to Dr. Cox, one elbow leaning a bit jauntily on the doctor's shoulder as he, too, peered at the baby. Then he turned to Pat and said, "Don't worry, Ma. Everything will be okay."

No sooner had he offered this reassurance than the spirit suddenly disappeared, and at that very moment the baby started to cry.

That dream was prophetic not only in indicating a problem at the moment of birth but also in foretelling the personality of David Coleman Beadle, born September 17, 1969, in Pocatello, Idaho. Even before his earthly life began, apparently, he was lively and curious, right in the thick of the action.

After the dream, Pat *knew* that this would be no ordinary birth and that there would be problems. Sure enough, two weeks later she was rushed to the hospital, where it was discovered that the baby was lying crosswise in the birth canal. After several attempts had been made to reposition him, he was pulled out feet first, which caused pressure on nerves that affected his motor skills. David was almost two years old before his eager spirit succeeded in teaching his body to walk.

But from that moment on he hardly paused for breath. There were too many exciting things to experience. Curious and hyperactive, David was a child who liked to explore.

Pat remembers putting him down for a nap as a toddler and thinking with a weary sigh that she could relax for a minute. No sooner had she put her feet up than she heard someone banging on the front door. A frantic neighbor screamed, "Did you know your little boy is climbing on your roof?"

Time passed, and it was August 23, 1973. David was three years old. Now they lived in Yuba City, California.

A new baby had joined the family in June, which Pat's mother agreed to babysit while Pat drove the other four children to the genealogy library in nearby Gridley. But as usual David was into everything, and she decided it was best to go home.

Pat parked the car in front of her parents' house and left the kids sitting there quietly while she ran inside to pick up the baby, cautioning them—especially David—not to move. But the baby was napping, and gathering up a sleeping baby, blankets, and diaper bag took an extra minute or two Pat hadn't counted on. During that moment, David and five-year-old Michael slipped out of the car, through the gate, and into the backyard.

Normally that excursion wouldn't have been so tragic. The children loved to play in the fenced yard, where their grandfather had all kinds of fascinating projects under way. But on this hot summer day David managed to climb to the top of a huge 8' x 8' outdoor workbench, where his grandfather stored his larger tools, a platform purposely raised high enough off the ground to keep prying little fingers from meddling.

Pat was walking toward the front door when David stumbled in through the back, white foam in evidence around his mouth. Her first impression was that he'd eaten a handful of her mother's detergent. It looked like soap, bubbling and frothing from his lips, but as he hurtled toward her, David whimpered, "Mouth *hurts!*"

Pat grabbed her son and tried to wash the foam away, then realized it wasn't foam after all but burned flesh, which on closer scrutiny reminded her of fried fish.

In reality he'd drunk a lethal dose of nitric acid laced with mercury.

After climbing the workbench, David had discovered a glass filled with a transparent liquid used by his grandfather to extract gold from sand and mercury out of the gold. The day was hot, and, thinking the glass held water, David raised it to his mouth and swallowed it.

Then began a series of what Pat calls "mini miracles." David was slipping into shock, so it was critical, she knew, that they reach the hospital without delay. Pat scooped her son into her arms and flew out to her car—at the precise moment when a policeman just happened to drive by. Before she could hail him, however, he drove on past, and the opportunity to solicit his help was gone.

Or was it? Suddenly a dog ran into the street directly in front of the patrol car, causing the policeman to slam on his brakes and stop, thus allowing the desperate mother to catch up and attract his attention. The officer ushered them into his own vehicle and, with siren screaming, raced them to the hospital. On his car radio he was able to call medical personnel to prepare them for the baby's arrival.

Another miracle. Dr. DeMatei was on duty that day, winding up his rounds in preparation for vacation the following morning. Of all the doctors on staff, Dr. DeMatei was the most qualified to handle an accident of this magnitude.

David's throat closed off and he was rushed to emergency, where they considered he had no chance to pull through. All that night doctors worked over him in a life-and-death situation.

His lips were burned to a crisp and puffed out grotesquely. A scar ran fierce and red from one corner of his mouth to his chin, silently pointing to where acid had dripped from his lips.

His kidneys shut down, so Dr. DeMatei ordered him transferred to a hospital in Sacramento where dialysis could be performed.

As one agonizing day followed another, Pat and Doug independently began to question whether they were doing what was right in the sight of the Lord. They were praying ceaselessly that David would live, of course. They thought they were saying, "Thy will be done," but did they mean it? Were their prayers holding their little boy back when it might be in the plan for him to go?

A strong impression came to Pat that they would receive an answer to their confusion of mind if their stake patriarch gave David a blessing. Before she mentioned the idea to her husband, Doug had had an identical impression and had already completed the arrangements.

Patriarch Hughes met with them on Friday night, and it appeared during the first two hours of conversation that he was preparing the grieving parents for the loss of their son.

He explained that the spirit world isn't a scary place, a spot to be dreaded or feared. He knew *that* positively from a personal near-death experience, and he related the story in detail. So when the blessing began, the Beadles fully expected the patriarch to release their beloved David to die.

That didn't happen. In the blessing he promised the boy that he would live, that he had a special mission to perform. Afterwards, he told them, in a voice filled with awe, "I have never experienced anything like this before—like an electrical shock passing through me to your son."

David lay in intensive care for five weeks with nurses by his bedside round the clock, hands tied down so he couldn't yank out the annoying tubes that led to various parts of his body.

Not a second of those weeks was easy. A tracheotomy allowed him to breathe but made it impossible to speak or utter any type of sound. Once the tube leading to his throat was somehow knocked slightly askew; the nurse heard it gurgling, thought the tube was blocked and, in attempting to clear it, pumped all the air from his lungs. Instantly David turned as black as a piece of coal, and at that moment his mother was certain he was gone.

But the resuscitation crew revived him.

He lost one third of his body weight because it was impossible for him to eat. Nourishment consisted of sugar water through an IV.

The brain damage doctors feared was probable because of the mercury he'd ingested didn't materialize, but they worried about permanent emotional trauma. When small children suffer terrible injuries, they frequently withdraw. Not connecting their agony with the accident and not understanding why they must endure such pain, they simply do not allow themselves to feel anything at all.

David showed classic symptoms of retreating within himself, into a space so deeply hidden from the world that he might never find his way back. He assumed the fetal position when he slept, and through all that long, frightening hospital ordeal, he never once shed a tear.

Pat spent hours drawing pictures of events leading to the accident so that he would know why he was there, as well as scenes depicting his treatment in the hospital so that he would understand what they were doing to him. She also made a tape of the entire Primary songbook, making it possible for him to listen to messages of hope and be comforted. She was touched when the songs also comforted David's nurses.

This child, scarcely more than a baby, celebrated his fourth birthday in the hospital, and that was where his brother and two sisters saw him for the first time since the accident.

A nurse helped him walk slowly and painfully across the room with tubes all over his body, eyes enormous in an emaciated face, and knees huge and knobby against the skin and bones of his legs. The other children were understandably frightened. Was this really their little brother? It took a while before they felt comfortable about giving him a hug.

Finally hospital officials felt they could risk sending him closer to home, back to the Yuba City Hospital for another three weeks. But somehow they sent him on a Sunday, without notifying his parents and without sending his records. And without authorization for ICU, he was placed in a regular room, still not able to talk or to ask for help of any kind.

By then David's food was blenderized and watered down and introduced to his body through a tube through his nose, a tube that was left in place twenty-four hours a day and held in place with tape across his cheek because his throat at the base of his tongue was so scarred that it required a major effort to replace the tube should it become dislodged.

He was alive and much improved, but he still needed constant watching to make sure he didn't pull out his tubes or get something caught in his tracheotomy.

When full-time nurses were not available, the Relief Society president scheduled ward people, from teenagers to grandparents, in four-hour shifts—even through the night —and they responded with unbelievable commitment. Two women were scheduled from 12:00 midnight to 4:00 A.M., and from 4:00 A.M. to 8:00 A.M. They had only one question: "Which hospital in Sacramento is David in?" Not realizing he had been moved back to Yuba City, they were willing to travel the fifty miles, at night, on a regular basis.

The hospital staff was amazed at how quickly David responded to the love these volunteers displayed. They nicknamed them the "Mormon Angels," since they truly performed miracles in David's emotional recovery.

Soon after David was able to return home, his mother squeezed his shoulders and said, "Heavenly Father sure does love you, David." His answer was, "I know that, because Jesus told me."

The boy went on to describe to his startled mother how Jesus had held him on his lap—"He was dressed in white and I had a red shirt." (Actually David's shirt at the time of the accident was bright orange, but his mother figured that was close enough for a child who was still young enough to be a little hazy about his colors.)

"Jesus told me I needed to go back, because I need to learn to be a good boy, learn to obey my parents, be baptized, and go on a mission. But don't worry, Mom. When I'm seventeen years old I will be able to eat with my mouth!"

Two months later the veil was drawn over this memory. David no longer recalls what he once described so vividly, except that he was left with the unshakable conviction that by the time he was seventeen he would eat with his mouth.

Another priesthood blessing, this time given by the stake president, confirmed that fact. Through the frustrating years of growing up that belief sustained him through some very difficult times.

Reaction of other children to his being *different* was perhaps one of the hardest crosses to bear. Eventually the nose tube was replaced with another tube implanted directly into his stomach, and the blended meals went in by way of a large syringe.

When David was old enough to attend school, he didn't feel like one of the regular guys, partly because he couldn't participate in sports. Every lunch hour and recess, instead of joining his classmates for fun and fellowship, he had to hurry to the nurse's office to "eat." Often the blenderized food spilled or leaked from the tube, irritating his skin and embarrassing the boy with food stains on his clothing.

Normal roughhousing, even at home with his brothers and sisters (eight, by then), might—and usually did—dislodge the tube. David constantly had to step back from physical fun, an action directly opposed to his natural inclination.

But consider the psychological impact of never putting cake or spaghetti or bread warm from the oven into one's mouth—*never* chewing or swallowing. David loved the taste of food—craved it—couldn't resist sneaking a bite now and again, chewing it up and spitting it out. The problem was that the slightest straying crumb or bit of thickened saliva ended up in his lungs, causing respiratory infection. Equally as many weeks were spent sick at home or in the hospital as at school.

No, David's life was definitely not easy. Neither was it easy for his parents.

The years passed in a blur of hospitals and surgery.

In 1974 doctors attempted to transplant part of the intestines to the throat. After fourteen hours of unsuccessful surgery his lungs collapsed and he developed chemical pneumonia. In addition they had nicked his vocal cord, and again he was left for six weeks without a voice.

One day Pat worked around the house while David played in a bedroom. She had no way of knowing he'd caught his finger in an exercise device. He tried to scream for help, but no sound would come. There was no escape until Pat happened into the room and came to his rescue. From then on his distraught mom insisted that he wear a whistle around his neck.

David's ability to produce sound did return. He speaks now in a whispery, gravelly voice—similar to President Spencer W. Kimball's after *his* surgery, about which he joked that he had fallen into the hands of cutthroats.

Slowly David's health improved, and he attended classes on a more regular basis. He filled all the requirements to become a full-fledged Eagle Scout and was an honor, straight-A student at school, taking solid courses like physics, German, and so on. His powerful spirit wouldn't let his physical disabilities interfere.

Always prominent in David's thoughts was his desire to fill a mission. His older brother, Mike, reached missionary age and was called to serve in the West Indies.

By now David was seventeen years old.

Pat and Doug drove Mike back to the MTC in Provo, Utah, in May and took David along. Several years earlier he had been treated in the Primary Children's Hospital in Salt Lake City, and they resolved to visit the doctors there one more time.

Dr. Johnson was head of the surgical department, and they walked into his office without an appointment. Would he remember them after so long? He did—remembered them well. And—wonder of wonders—with great excitement he told them that five of the world's top specialists in the area of ear, nose, and throat were meeting that summer at the University of Utah! Dr. Johnson arranged for an examination for David.

They operated in August—David was still seventeen—twenty-two hours of intense, mind-boggling, and unique micro-surgery in which this time they were able to successfully transplant intestinal tissue to the throat.

They cut him from ear to ear, from chin to naval, and across his abdomen from hip to hip. In addition, wavy incisions from elbows to wrists on both inner arms permitted extraction of healthy veins to attach to the new throat passage, keeping it well supplied with healing blood.

A scar under the ribs from earlier surgery circled from mid-stomach to mid-back. Later on one doctor shook his head as he examined David and muttered, "I've never seen so many scars—except on a body after an autopsy."

The surgery was more than touchy. It carried a real possibility of death, and David knew that in advance. He and his mother spent most of the night before the operation analyzing and weighing every possibility. The boy was still adamant.

"I want to go on a mission," he said, "and I can't do that lugging a blender. So what if I don't make it through? I can fill my mission on the other side."

After it was over, nurses questioned their patient: "Why would anyone voluntarily go through such an ordeal? You came to grips with your situation years ago. Wouldn't it have been easier to continue the way you were?"

David grinned and said, "It may have been easier, but I doubt if my companions could have handled it. Think of all the dinner appointments they'd have had to give up!"

Learning to allow himself to swallow has been difficult for David psychologically. Remembering the bad times when he was ill with so many infections, it took all the courage he could muster to consciously let food slip down his throat. For years a child small in stature due to lack of normal nourishment, now he has grown to an impressive five feet nine.

In David's first interview after receiving his call and reporting to his mission field, President Fox was naturally a little apprehensive as to what this new missionary's limitations might be. As he read David's medical background those fears became more apparent, until finally David grinned and replied, "President, don't worry about me. I have *lots* of grit!"

David entered the Wisconsin Milwaukee Mission on September 7, 1989, successfully accomplishing his heart's desire—and what he has known his Heavenly Father wanted him to do since he was three years old.

6

Let Your Hearts Be Comforted

Trusting the scriptures became a habit early in the life of JoAnn Barrett Gray.

The oldest of a sizeable family, she remembers how her parents gathered all eleven children around the table in their farmhouse in Idaho, how under her father's direction they searched out and studied the holy words of God.

The amazing thing to JoAnn as a child was how often her parents picked the very scripture to solve a problem in their children's lives. Their knowledge of exactly where to find counsel a family member needed was impressive.

JoAnn and Gary continued turning to the scriptures regularly in their own home, with their own three children —Christine, small, dark-haired, with a keen, serious mind like her father's; Steven, strong, sturdy, all boy; and Marilyn, tall, willowy, with hair as fair as her sister Christine's was dark. Three so different in appearance, and yet each one so dear.

When the children were very small JoAnn and Gary read them stories from the Bible. As teenagers they opened their own books around the table after dinner. Each took his or her turn speaking the words aloud, and then lively discussions pinpointed how they felt about what they had read. These were priceless hours of closeness and love.

All too soon the children grew up, married, and moved away, establishing their own homes and starting their own little families.

Sadly, none of us is immune to tragedy. In November 1984 Christine lost her valiant fight with cancer, a struggle she waged for eighteen months and at one point seemed to have won. In the end she left not only her grieving parents and brother and sister, but a desolate husband and three helpless babies, the youngest a scant two years old.

Stunned with grief, JoAnn and Gary clung together and held tightly to their faith as to a lifeline. Losing Christine was almost impossibly hard to bear, but with God's help they would learn to accept it.

Five months later their grief was compounded by truly unbelievable news. Steven had been killed—instantly—in a car crash.

Psychiatrists warn that the gravest danger associated with stress is heaping a second tragedy onto the first, without opportunity to properly heal. Two of their three children were gone—in only five short months! Was that *possible?* Neighbors and friends worried that the double blow might be more than the Grays could handle, and if they buckled under the load, who could blame them?

Yet somehow they did handle it. Keeping busy helped. Throwing themselves into their jobs during the week and into Church callings on Sundays filled enough of the void that at least they could walk through the motions of living, to keep up appearances. Perhaps, in time, some measure of inner comfort would return.

On April 21, 1985, a month after Steven's accident, JoAnn told herself she had buried her sorrow reasonably well, considering.

It was Sunday. She dutifully attended ward conference in one of the sister wards, in her capacity as Young Women secretary in the stake.

She drove home after the meeting was over, arriving before her husband did, and stepped into a house that was empty—and silent—and cold.

Unfortunately, not quite empty. Sorrow lurked behind the front door and its presence overwhelmed her completely, attacking so suddenly and viciously that she was powerless to fight it off alone.

With a fresh burst of agony every bit as raw as it had been in the beginning, JoAnn faced honestly the loneliness of life without two of her children, and acknowledged for the first time that the comfort she yearned for with her whole soul had not come.

Her pain was so overwhelming that she threw herself on the bed, arms stretched out, sobs racking her body, and cried in anguish, "Oh, my children, my children! How can I go on without you?"

Finally, when the worst of the hysteria passed, she knelt in great weariness at the side of the bed in prayer. She pleaded for only one thing.

"Heavenly Father, I have always tried to do what you would ask of me. Now I am desperate and I need your help. I *need* some assurance that Christine and Steven are with you, that they are happy and well. Please, *please* let them come to me for just a minute. Let me feel their touch just once—*please* Father—that in my mother's heart I might know they are all right."

In this attitude of humility she waited, motionless, alert, for a lengthy period of time, willing the veil to part enough for some small contact.

Nothing happened. Nothing at all.

Exhausted, JoAnn rose to her feet, not bitter, but understanding instinctively that the miracle she begged for would not be hers. She must—and perhaps even could—endure to the end on the basis of the faith she already had.

But because the habit was ingrained, she groped on the nightstand for her scriptures. She would read to pass the time until Gary's car sounded in the driveway.

The volume fell open in her hands. Not to the front or center pages as books usually do when moving naturally on their own, but close to the end. Her eyes still brimmed with tears as she blinked and tried to focus on the words:

"Therefore, let your hearts be comforted concerning Zion; for all flesh is in mine hands; be still and know that I am God" (D&C 101:16).

Be still and know that I am God! That was her answer. Her children were all right, in a heaven where those who have passed on are busy and well, and she was filled with the inexpressible comfort of that knowledge.

She no longer needs to waste time searching for answers to questions that are already answered.

Heavenly Father is taking care of us all.

7

First Edition

*

Good deeds planted in fertile soil are seldom lost. Sometimes they are harvested after a lifetime of incubation.

As a teacher, Larry Stapley of Fair Oaks, California, owns a lot of books. His favorite is an old, weatherbeaten first edition of the Book of Mormon—one of the original five thousand copies printed by E. B. Grandin at Palmyra in 1830.

"This book is my prized possession," he said, as he carefully removed it from a wooden box and unwound the towel that protects it. Its pages are yellowed and stained as if it has rested in the rafters of someone's attic on a rainy day. And perhaps it did just that.

Larry was twenty-four years old when he was converted to The Church of Jesus Christ of Latter-day Saints. A year later, to the day, he was called to serve a mission for his new church. He was excited! He hadn't expected that opportunity, because his parents were not financially able to support him on a mission. Then "Uncle Del" (Apostle) Stapley —not related, but a close and dear friend—offered to pay his expenses.

In the small town of Clay Center, Kansas, Larry and his new companion dropped in at the local library. They passed the time of day with Miss Miller, the librarian, then checked the religion shelf for a copy of the Book of Mormon. If the library didn't have one on display, Elder Stapley planned to donate one of his own.

The card catalog indicated there was such a book in stock. Not a new, shiny edition, but an old issue printed in 1830. Afraid to even hope that it just *might* be what he suspected, Elder Stapley checked it out and hurried home to compare the book's title page with a picture he'd seen in his copy of *Essentials in Church History*. The book and the picture were identical; the book was authentic.

"I was almost too excited to breathe," he recalls. "We rushed back to the library and explained to the librarian what she had. I told her this was quite a valuable book, although probably more valuable to members of our church than to anyone else. Only one other person had checked it out in all the years it had lain forgotten on the shelf. I asked if I could buy it."

Miss Miller was surprisingly obliging. She called every member of the board personally, and they all agreed that the eager young man was welcome to the book. She waited until last to call the minister of the largest Protestant church in Clay Center, a man who had been friendly only until the missionaries had baptized one of the pillars of his congregation.

But, also surprisingly, the minister too agreed, and for the voluntary price of one new Book of Mormon, one Doctrine and Covenants, and one *Jesus the Christ*, the exchange was made.

How did this treasure find its way to the shelves of the Clay Center Public Library? Miss Miller, then a spinster of some seventy years, had begun work at the library as a young, inexperienced girl. Before long the board sent her to faraway Salt Lake City, Utah, to attend a library conference.

She was impressed with the beauty of the wide streets, the cleanliness she saw there, and the pure water rushing down the sparkling gutters.

She was particularly pleased by the friendliness of the Mormon people. On early morning walks, so far from home, she was greeted kindly by everyone she passed.

Years later she was authorized to look over a huge supply of books left at the death of her town's leading citizen, to personally decide which volumes were worth keeping and which should be destroyed. Most showed signs of irreversible neglect. She dropped the old, weatherbeaten Book of Mormon onto the floor, with all of the others she had planned to discard.

Then a vivid picture of Salt Lake City all those years ago popped into her mind. She remembered the love shown to a young, lonely girl by the people who lived there, and somehow she couldn't bring herself to throw away this particular worn-out volume. She reached down to the floor to salvage it.

At the end of his labors, Elder Stapley offered the book to Elder Stapley the Apostle. The latter had paid for the mission, and in all fairness this priceless possession should belong to him. But "Uncle Del" refused. He said, "Larry, it was your mission. You found the book. It's yours."

And sure enough, that's what the card in the front pocket still indicates. Written in a firm hand, directly underneath the date—31 Mar., 1955—is:

Donated to Elder Stapley.

Leone B. Miller, Clay Center, Kansas.

8

I Must Go Back!

Patriarchs are exceptional men.

The ones I know have been special all their lives, conducting their temporal affairs as honorably as if they strode with one foot on earth and one already in heaven, unusually spiritual people even before they were patriarchs. Perhaps that inborn integrity is what *leads* to their holy calling.

Patriarch George D. Hughes—who put his hands on the head of little David Beadle and promised the boy that he would live—was no exception.

He was born in Spanish Fork, Utah, on the shores of Utah Lake, in 1898.

Early in life he was recognized as being special. As he entered high school, two of the best law firms in Salt Lake City contacted him to offer him a tempting position should he decide on the study of law. He liked that suggestion, and he took four years of Latin, three years of Spanish, and two years of debating. He thought he was on his way.

But World War I and illness as a result of the war changed his plans. He came home in bad shape, physically, undergoing hospital treatments daily while attending college. Even so, he completed a four-year accounting course in two and a half years, carrying twenty-five hours of solid classes.

Graduating from the University of Utah, he was offered and accepted a teaching position as assistant professor in the college's accounting department.

Later he moved to Berkeley to study for his doctorate at the University of California. While there he taught advanced accounting and the laws of taxation, as a full professor.

He lived for a time in Berkeley and became a partner with John F. Forbes and Company. As a member of the firm he did estate tax and account planning for William Randolph Hearst, the famous and influential newspaper publisher.

Brother Hughes was involved when the church negotiated with the Hearst family to acquire property for the Berkeley Institute of Religion.

He transferred to Honolulu, Hawaii, in 1964 to manage the firm's Honolulu office, teaching courses there in the laws of taxation. He taught the same courses later at Golden Gate College (now Golden Gate University) in San Francisco.

He was a beloved counselor in the bishopric of my brother-in-law Allan Mackay's ward in Menlo Park, California, and in later life a patriarch in the Yuba City area, plus a temple worker on Wednesdays and Thursdays in the Oakland Temple.

With that background as to the calibre of man he was, it's time to move on to his electrifying war experiences.

Three nights before the United States entered the war in April, 1917, George Hughes had a vision of himself as a soldier in a blue uniform. It wasn't a dream but an actual vision, a flash of foreknowledge, and he saw himself returning home alive. The next morning he related to his mother what he had seen, and on April 6 he enlisted in the Marine Corps, donning the very uniform that in the vision he had seen himself wear.

By early July he was sent overseas, and he ended up in Belleau Woods in France, on a wooded hill in a perfectly level area called Boursches wheat fields. He was attached to a regiment in the Second Division of the American Expeditionary Forces. His outfit helped stop the German army in its drive toward Paris.

George was very angry that day because many of his fellow soldiers and close friends had been shot. Down the hill he could clearly see lines of German soldiers bearing Maxim machine guns invented in the United States, weapons refused by the American military but used to terrible advantage by the enemy. Their guns were set up on tripods, and the tripods were so numerous that they touched each other for what seemed to stretch on for miles.

George was a sniper—a marksman who could hit a circle the size of a silver dollar at 500 yards, five times out of five. A telescopic sight on his rifle enabled him to blast small targets at far distances.

Just before dawn he secretly made his way to a sheltered spot where he expected to do some sniping. Crawling along the ground, he heard somebody cry for help. He stopped to listen, and decided the sound must have come from a shell hole down the hill and only ten yards in front of an active German machine gun nest. He pinpointed the distance by fire from the enemy guns.

He watched, his heart in his throat, wondering what to do, while rays of early morning sun lit up a white hand groping out of the hole, and again came that pitiful cry for help. He whispered to himself, "I'm sorry, soldier. We can't get you out of there. It's impossible." Then he felt a touch on his shoulder and heard a voice say, "Only you can, George. Only you."

George crawled back to Lieutenant Hal N. Potter and requested permission to attempt the rescue. The lieutenant refused. Anyone foolish enough to volunteer would be moving directly toward the murderous enemy guns, a perfect target. The attempt would be suicide.

George said, "Lieutenant, I'm telling you I *can* go get that soldier and come back." He was so insistent that against his better judgment the officer relented.

Word was passed along American lines that when Sgt. Hughes started down the hill, all guns were to fire as a diversionary action. He jumped out of the trench and jogged down the hill—and every enemy gun also opened up, including those in the forbidding nest closest to the soldier he hoped to reach.

He fixed his eyes on the point of fire and saw bullets streaking out of the guns. Lots of bullets. Headed straight for him. Peculiarly, not one of them touched his body. Strafing kicked up dirt and debris all around him, as if someone had trained a water hose onto a lawn covered with leaves.

George dropped into the shell hole. There, frighteningly still, lay the form of a boy with a bloody wound in his right leg, which had been wrapped with raw salted pork or sowbelly before the soldier passed out. George threw the unconscious man over his shoulder, climbed out of the hole and looked directly into the eyes of the enemy. He said, "Guten morgen. Wie Gehen Sie?" And laughed.

The Germans sat frozen at their guns as if they were paralyzed, while George scanned the area for a way back to his camp. The hill wasn't high, but the man on his back weighed at least two hundred pounds. George wasn't sure his legs could make it. Finally he spotted a kind of rivulet, made his way up that indentation, and with his free right hand balanced his weight against the dirt.

In eerie silence he struggled up the hill and reached the safety of the trenches. Two other men leaped up to pull the soldier off his back as George rolled over and screamed out, "Hit the deck!" Just as he dived to the ground, the Germans opened up again. Every machine gun in the vicinity shot at them. Unfortunately his two courageous helpers were wounded, but not fatally.

From then on George's buddies called him "Sgt. Bulletproof." And not without further cause. For months he led his troops to the very edges of hell, and no bullet touched him. George, himself, came to believe he was invincible.

That belief was the reason he was so surprised at the next incident.

On July 19, 1918, Sgt. Hughes returned from a reconnaisance mission. Spotting an abandoned foxhole, he crawled into it to sleep. It wasn't deep. Apparently someone had interrupted digging when his shovel struck a huge rock. But the space was large enough for a man to snuggle in below the surface of the ground. He hadn't eaten anything decent for days. Tired and hungry, George stretched out on his stomach in the hole and immediately went to sleep.

When he awoke, he was surprised to find himself standing in a well-lit, spacious room. He was puzzled because there was no lamp or electrical appliance that he could detect.

A man in white approached him, and George hesitatingly said, "I presume I'm in the spirit world." The man assured him his presumption was correct, while handing George some clothing of fabric that was wonderfully white. Obviously he expected the new arrival to dress himself in the clothes.

George thought that would be a waste of time. He knew he couldn't stay. The only reason his mother had permitted him to join the service in the first place was that he had solemnly promised her he would return. He had seen himself return in the vision. He earnestly questioned the man before him: "Can you give me permission to go back?" The answer was, "No, I cannot." George insisted, "Then take me to someone who can."

They left the original building together and came out on a park, a breathtaking spot with lawns, trees, bushes, and flowers. They walked along the edge of the park, passing buildings on the right with the park on their left. Other individuals crossed the park diagonally, following a smaller footpath. George noticed they all seemed to be between thirty-five and forty-five years of age, and they all walked with purpose.

Following his guide's lead, he entered a second building where three men sat around a large, beautiful table. George spoke to the personage in the center and pleaded to be allowed to return. The man said, "You surely couldn't *want* to go back—not to that place of war and dirt?"

So George told him about the vision, explained how he had studied every poster at the recruiting office until he located a sandwich board bearing the picture of a handsome marine in a blue uniform—identical to the one he saw himself wearing in the vision; how he'd called his mother from the recruiter's phone when he was told he was too young to join without parental consent; how she *had* consented on the strength of the vision and his assurance that he would return to her alive.

George was puzzled about how he came to be in the spirit world. He said, "I don't know how this happened. The last thing I remember was lying down to go to sleep."

The center man, obviously the spokesman, furnished details. A bomb had exploded over the foxhole and many young men in the vicinity had been killed. They were casualties in an accident of war.

George used every bit of his training in debate. He listed every reason he could think of as to why he should return to earth. He appreciated the spirit world, or the part of it he had now seen. It was lovely, a place he looked forward with great anticipation to calling home eventually, and certainly earthly worries and the sins prompted by Satan were clearly not there. Yet he knew that this time he couldn't stay.

The spokesman listened and shook his head. He couldn't fathom why anyone would choose to go back, but he agreed to look into the possibility. In the meantime, George's guide could show him around.

George noticed that everyone they met spoke the same language, and he understood it with ease, although he didn't remember hearing it spoken before. The guide impressed on him the importance—if he did go back—of not divulging details of what he would see. It didn't appear to be objectionable if he spoke generally of the meeting with the three officials, or the argument he had put up to return.

After a time they went back to the men, and the center one again did the communicating. He asked, "Surely you don't still want to go back?" When he saw that George felt compelled, he turned to the guide and said, "Go ahead and take him."

George and the guide walked out of the building and down a long, deserted street. There was nobody in sight. And suddenly they were traveling through the air at a tremendous speed. He saw the earth appear as a tiny black dot, then expand before them like an image from a camera with a zoom lens. The whole trip was completed in a matter of seconds.

They dropped down closer and he could see the battlefield. Then the guide pointed his finger and said, "There's your shell hole."

George looked, and saw a jagged gash now eight or ten yards in diameter. Twenty forms lay unmoving around the sides of the excavation, wrapped in sheets or blankets and tied at each end. A group of workers bustled about, busily carrying stretchers to transport the forms to another location.

A doctor with a stethoscope hanging around his neck examined the contents of the bundles. When bodies were intact he used his stethoscope to listen in vain for a heartbeat. He pulled eyelids back to scrutinize dead eyes, shook his head, and in every case hung on the bodies a dated and signed tag reading "Death Confirmed."

As George continued to watch, a bundle was opened to reveal a complete body, and in shock George exclaimed, "Hey, that's me!" He watched the doctor write pertinent data on the tag, rewrap the body, and turn it over to the others for burial.

A grave had been dug a quarter of a mile away—a long, common grave six feet deep. Bodies were laid side by side, heads in one direction and feet in another. Two black men, one on each side of the grave, were pushing bodies together tightly and covering them with dirt.

(A check with the military confirmed for me that this unusual procedure was used in Civil War and World War I battles when casualties were horrendous in number. Later the dead were dug up and reburied in solitary plots with appropriate markers, or shipped back home to relatives.)

George watched from above and was fascinated! Suddenly he heard his guide say, "George—look! You have to hurry!"

Dirt was being shoveled on top of *his* body. By then it was a foot or more deep.

He can't remember exactly how he re-entered his body. His spirit just shot in with a whoosh, and there he was, inside of a blanket tied at both ends, feeling the thud of clods of dirt falling on top of him. He could still wriggle, and he pulled his feet up as hard as he could. He bent his knees and struggled. One of the men noticed movements under the mound of earth. Dropping to his knees, he pawed at the dirt. Others joined in, and soon George's "body" was brushed off and unwrapped.

He read the information on the tag, which said: *George D. Hughes, 20th Company, 5th Regiment, American Expeditionary Forces. Death confirmed July 22.*

July 22? He had lain down to sleep on July 19. Apparently his spirit had been separated from his body the night of the nineteenth, all day and night of the twentieth, day and night of the twenty-first, and reunited today—the day of confirmation of his death—on July 22. And yet where he'd been he'd seen no darkness at all.

He was weak but able to walk. Someone pointed him in the direction of the Second Division, and he started off to find them. When he staggered in, one of the men in the platoon was washing his mess kit. George reached in from behind him, took the pot of hot water out of his hand, and begged, "Please, let me have that. And I've got to have some food."

The thunderstruck marine screamed, "Sergeant Hughes!" Men came running from every direction, knowing they had seen their buddy killed. George and Captain Martineau hadn't been close personal friends, but the captain threw his arms around George's shoulders in a giant bear hug. (George wasn't sure at the time whether this was done in relief at seeing him alive or as a test to be certain he wasn't a ghost.)

They sent for the doctor who traveled with the corps, and he worked George over while George stood there gulping down food. A kerosene bath and a hot shower were next on the agenda, because he was filthy, of course. Three days and nights of lying dead in the field had taken their toll. He was driven by ambulance to the military hospital, where he was put to sleep between clean, white, luxurious sheets, with caring nurses hovering over him.

George D. Hughes was awarded the Distinguished Service Cross from the army for extraordinary heroism against an armed enemy (his regiment had been affiliated with the army for a time); the Navy Cross; the Second Division Citation; the Marine Corps Good Conduct Medal; and five French regimental citations. The Army and Navy crosses are second only to the Congressional Medal of Honor.

George arrived in New York on March 3, 1919, and went to Quantico, Virginia, for additional medical treatment for his lungs, which had been badly gassed.

He was honorably discharged in April, 1919, resuming a life that was no less remarkable from that day on until his second death in 1980, at the age of eighty-two.

9

The Irresistible Urge

Lightning never strikes twice in the same place. That's what they say, although in truth those familiar words may be an old wives' tale without substance.

The Spirit, however, is another matter, and it carries no such restrictions.

Laura and Brent Whitaker's application to adopt another child had been filed with the Church adoption agency for approximately a year. Their precious little Dawn was three and a half now, and for quite some time they had felt a yearning for another baby. Each time their thoughts returned to the strange and wonderful night when Dawn was born,* the need for a second baby grew stronger.

Adoptions are not completed as quickly as young prospective parents might wish. This time Brent and Laura

---

*See chapter 14 of the author's book *The Outstretched Arms*, Bookcraft, 1983.

were told it could take as long as three years. Though they'd waited for months already, names of other equally eager couples had been on the list much, much longer.

Dawn was a tiny, delicate child, one who still fit into her crib with ease. She was contented sleeping there, and Laura was constantly surprised that never once did she attempt to climb out by herself. Even with the side of the crib pushed down, Dawn stayed put until Laura lifted her out.

The thought occurred to Laura—and then became more insistent—that when the new baby did arrive, they could have a problem. For several weeks she had considered shopping for another bed and making the change. It seemed logical that Dawn might resist leaving the crib. What a shame if they didn't allow sufficient time to wean her from her special spot before it was usurped by a stranger!

Laura carried those thoughts tucked vaguely away in the back of her mind, but there was no urgency. After all, many more months or even years would pass before the new baby came and moved into the crib.

One morning Laura was dusting in the living room when she thought of the rollaway bed normally stored in the garage. A friend had borrowed it earlier, but it was back now. Why wait to purchase a bed? They could do that later. Why not set up the rollaway, temporarily, in Dawn's room —today?

She pushed the rollaway to the bedroom door and left it waiting there while she shoved the crib into a corner. Then she unfolded the bed and spread it out on the spot where the crib had rested for all of Dawn's life. She tucked the sheets neatly in at the corners, added a quilt or two, and finished it off with a colorful bedspread and pillow.

Finally, she stepped back to survey her handiwork. It looked inviting to her, but how would it appear to Dawn? Laura wouldn't be too surprised if her daughter's emotional transition to the bed took the better part of a month, but they had plenty of time.

But they didn't have months or years to effect the change. Dawn took to the new bed right away, and it was a good thing she did. Five days later the Whitaker's brand new baby boy was sleeping in the discarded crib.

Is there a list in heaven that links adoptive children and their new parents, even before the agencies make that decision themselves?

The thing that makes this story remarkable is that for the Whitakers, lightning *did* strike twice. Three and a half years earlier Brent had kept an entire dinner party waiting, and gourmet food grew cold while he wandered up and down the aisles of several stores buying baby furniture they didn't yet need, an act that was uncharacteristically rude. All this on the very night when Dawn was in the process of being born. Even Brent didn't understand his compulsive behavior until six weeks later when they were contacted by the agency.

Likewise, little Tommy came to earth on the exact day when Laura felt an unexpected but irresistible urge to prepare for his coming.

10

Imbisbuhlstrasse Seben

The travel folder *promised* us that "Switzerland is as safe as being rocked in your mother's arms." Then why was I so terrified?

Nobody in the family was more excited than I was when my husband, Ed, called from work to say there was a possibility he might be sent to Zurich for a year and a half. Should he accept the assignment? Ed claims I started packing before he said good-by or hung up the phone.

Imagine—eighteen unbelievable months in a setting straight out of a fairytale! Think of the new friends we would make—and the adventures! I strongly encouraged him to accept.

We arrived at the Zurich airport, exhausted and grimy, after a long, round-the-clock flight from California. Sixteen-year-old Gayle and I were in slacks, rumpled by traveling. Ed and our son Steve, eighteen, hadn't shaved. Ronnie, seven, too young for stubble, was the only member of the family who looked halfway presentable.

It was Sunday morning when we arrived. Two months earlier we'd called a Swiss stake president for tips on living conditions in his small but fabulous country, and he'd kindly offered to search for a suitable apartment. And he had found one perfect for our needs, an unusual place where everything imaginable was furnished and waiting. Cabinets were built-in in the kitchen, dining room, and bathroom, an unheard-of arrangement in Switzerland.

Without hesitation, and never having seen us in person, President Hans Ringger drew money from his own pocket to secure the apartment until we could get there.

Missionaries greeted us at the airport and loaded our suitcases into the mission van. We were aghast to hear they planned to drive us to stake conference, where President Ringger was conducting. Our apartment key lay snugly in the president's pocket; and besides, he wanted to meet us.

Tiptoeing into that beautiful church halfway through the meeting to join clean, nicely-pressed Latter-day Saints in *our* state of disarray was not, we felt, the best way to present ourselves, but we were happy to find that nobody seemed to mind. That was our introduction to the friendship and understanding Latter-day Saints share wherever they happen to meet.

After conference, President Ringger and his missionaries escorted us to the suburb of Hoengg and showed us around the apartment. We were delighted with everything we saw. Hoengg is an older section of Zurich, and all of Imbisbuhlstrasse was quaint.

Our building was four stories high, very narrow, typical old-Swiss architecture. A furniture company occupied the ground floor; a government office used half of the second; we had the other half of the second and all of the third, with entry and main living quarters on the third. A family from Italy rented the fourth.

This was exactly the Switzerland our imaginations had conjured up back in America. Better, if anything. No doubt about it—we were in for the adventure of a lifetime!

Only one thing was lacking. We noticed there wasn't a bite of food in the cabinets. Not a crumb. That wasn't cause for concern until a missionary informed us that all of Switzerland closes on Sunday. It was two-thirty in the afternoon, and we were already famished.

None of us mentioned our pangs of hunger. We didn't want to appear ungrateful, because, after all, President Ringger had done so much. Amazing, when all he knew about us was that we are active members of the Church and that at the time Ed was ward clerk.

Hungry as we were, sleep was our priority. Ed and I settled the children in their respective rooms. Steve took the bedroom off the third floor entry; Gayle chose one of two rooms on the second floor, reached by a charming circular staircase. Ronnie set his toys up neatly in the adjoining second-floor room.

The master bedroom lay between the living room and the kitchen. Tired out by long hours and excitement, we all fell asleep right away.

I woke with a start to the most excruciating, unreasonable terror I've ever experienced.

What could possibly be wrong? We were settled in peaceful, well-ordered Switzerland, in the quietest of neighborhoods. Yet my stomach churned. Waves of heat emanated from my body. Had I contracted some dread tropical disease?

Why did my hysterical mind repeat over and over: *We can't stay here! We'll be destroyed!*

I slipped soundlessly from the bed and tiptoed to the living room to pace the floor while Ed slept, attempting to force myself to regain control.

What insanity possessed me? I was the one who had urged almost to the point of insistence that we come. How could I tell my husband now that we had to leave?

Nevertheless my thoughts whirled, feverishly charting a way to convince him that we must—*must*—move to a hotel this very evening, and stay in the country itself only long enough for one of his colleagues to replace us.

I heard footsteps from the bedroom and Ed appeared, rubbing sleep from his eyes. As soon as he reached me and wrapped me in his arms, the unreasoning terror was gone.

Loosened from its grip, I was embarrassed. What *had* set me off like that? I'm not a nervous, unstable person, and I pride myself on thinking logically. I like to make sense, and my irrational behavior for the last ten or fifteen minutes obviously didn't fall into that category. Then and there I decided not to give Ed a hint of my foolish fear.

We agreed we'd better locate food or face a most uncomfortable night. At 5:00 P.M. Ed roused Steve to tell him we were leaving, planning to haunt the neighborhood for that one store or restaurant that might be open. Steve fervently wished us luck and we left.

Luck was with us. Barely a block away we saw signs of life in a pub-like establishment. We went in, sat at a table, and stared blankly at a menu that could as well have been printed in Greek. It was German, of course, and neither of us could make out a word.

The waiter was friendly and anxious to oblige, but when we hopefully asked, "Do you speak English?" he shook his head and said, "Nein." That we understood. He raised his voice for a general plea for help, but nobody in the restaurant spoke English. (We learned later that almost no one in Hoengg speaks English. Our adventure had truly begun.)

But we knew there was food on the premises, and we couldn't go back to the kids empty-handed. There had to be a way.

Our eyes fell on posters hung on the wall, and one picture looked remarkably like a ham sandwich. We gestured and pointed, and counted out five on our fingers, then walked a few steps towards the door pretending to carry a sack, to indicate (we hoped) that we didn't want to eat them there.

Ordering drinks was considerably easier. We lifted imaginary glasses to our lips, but we said our own "Nein!" when the waiter suggested beer. (Fortunately *beer* and *bier* sound virtually the same.)

We walked out victoriously, carrying five delicious ham sandwiches and five cartons of cold chocolate milk.

Our evening back at the apartment was full of anticipation as we ate and spoke of excursions to the grocery store the next day, or perhaps a stroll to the corner to board the peerless tram for our first ride into town. We pored excitedly over our travel book and couldn't wait to see all the wonders it listed.

Bedtime for us came fairly early. The beds were comfortable, all set up with Federdeckes—plump feather covers we promptly dubbed "the big white marshmallows." Soft and cozy, again they lulled us into warm, wonderful sleep.

Until 2:30 A.M.

Again I woke suddenly, violently, with the same horrible dread and *knowledge* of destruction. Again I was burning up. Waves of heat seemed to consume my body with the same conviction: *We can't stay! We've got to escape from this place—tonight!*

My hand reached out to grope blindly for Ed, but before my fingers touched his shoulder the panic was gone. A sweet feeling of peace took its place. Again, I was puzzled and embarrassed. Was I losing my mind? I went back to sleep and slept soundly until 7:30 A.M.

Steve was perched on the edge of our bed when I opened my eyes. The expression on his face was guarded.

"Did you sleep well?" he asked, with what appeared to be a conscious effort to be casual. Ed yawned and stretched and said, "Like a baby! How about you?" Steve answered, "Fine. Fine!" But something in his tone was entirely too hearty to ring true.

Was it possible I wasn't the only one to be disturbed? I questioned Steve, but cautiously. I didn't want to plant fears in his mind in case I was mistaken about his expression. I did admit I'd slept very well indeed except for one small stretch toward morning. Had Steve noticed anything unusual? If so, I really wanted to hear about it.

By this time Ed was thoroughly confused.

Steve has always been special, a sensitive, spiritual child from the beginning. His study and grasp of the scriptures at an early age astounded us. Ordained an elder before we left our home in America, he'd gone through the temple in Oakland, and he would be in Europe only until his nineteenth birthday.

In five months he would be called to serve a mission for his Heavenly Father, and he could hardly wait. His whole life had been geared in that direction.

Now I sensed he was gripped by inner conflict. "You'll think I'm imagining things," he said. But then he described in detail his nocturnal experience with terror that I, too, had dealt with—twice.

Sound asleep, he had roused abruptly to the absolute *certainty* that if he didn't leave the apartment he would be destroyed. His thoughts were consumed with the idea of escape. Under the same faceless dread that I had felt in the master bedroom, he doubted whether he could make it through the front door alive.

Gradually our son recognized that he was wrestling with the spirit of evil itself. Why? Our family had never felt the reality of that presence in person and at that point had never spoken to anyone who had. In fact, hearing the story from somebody else's lips, we might have been inclined to politely scoff.

Now we both had assurance that the awful power was real. We weren't scoffing on that snowy February morning, and by then Ed wasn't, either.

As it had appeared to Steve that he was totally without hope, he recalled his priesthood, so recently bestowed. Silently he commanded the fearful entity to leave, and the blackness did ebb for a moment. Then it returned, stronger than ever.

Steve sprang from his bed and spoke out loud this time, raising his hand toward heaven: "With the power of the Melchizedek Priesthood which I hold, I command you to depart!" Immediately the force that had gripped him was gone, and he slipped back into bed and fell into exhausted sleep.

Listening intently, I was convinced that at that precise moment I had been released from my own fear.

But mortal minds acknowledge interference by supernatural powers only grudgingly. In the clear light of morning, one tries to come up with logical explanations. Could anything so diabolical *really* have happened? Or could my son and I merely have had bouts of coincidental "uneasiness" due to jet lag or fatigue?

We gathered the younger children together and knelt as a family around the living room couch, while Ed dedicated our home. We were careful not to mention the activities of the night to Gayle and Ronnie. Whatever had disturbed our sleep was gone now and best forgotten.

That night we were surprised when Ronnie objected to going to bed. He loved his room and spent hours playing, during the day, with favorite toys or reading at the child-sized table and chair. Now, after dark, he invented excuses not to go near the stairs.

The next night his anxiety increased.

Gayle and Ronnie had both gone to bed. A few minutes later Gayle's plaintive voice floated up to us from the stairwell. "Mother, would you come down for a minute?" she begged. I jumped up from the couch and hurried down the steps.

"It's silly, I know," she said hesitantly, "but I'm frightened when I'm down here at night." That struck me as odd because, like Ronnie, Gayle enjoyed her room and spent happy hours there with her oil paints—during the day. "Will you sit with me and hold my hand until I fall asleep?"

What was she afraid of? I asked her, but she didn't know.

I suggested having her older brother change beds with Ronnie for the night and she quickly agreed. Steve's being in the adjoining room might help her to relax.

The next morning Steve described the same scenario as before. Roused in the night, he felt the familiar, oppressive terror. This time he quickly called on his priesthood powers for protection and, leaving nothing to chance, made it clear that in the name of his Savior he banished evil from every room in the house. From the basement where we did our laundry. From the stairs leading to the apartment. From every inch of the small surrounding property.

Was our tormentor really gone? Could we be sure? We expected to have proof one way or another when bedtime rolled around again.

Almost from the moment we stepped foot into the apartment, Ronnie hadn't gone to bed willingly. If some unearthly power had in fact tried to intimidate us and now it was really gone, Ron should notice its absence. Ed, Steve, and I could hardly wait for eight-thirty.

Finally the clock in the old church tower a block away pealed the half-hour. I sang out, "Eight-thirty, Sweetie —time for bed," and held my breath.

After family prayer, Ronnie scooped up his crayons and coloring book, kissed us goodnight all around, and cheerfully skipped off down the stairs. Never again did he strenuously object to bedtime. Strange as it still seemed, we had our answer.

Several evenings later I questioned Gayle. Was she still nervous in her bedroom at night? She looked as embarrassed as I had felt. "Heavens no, Mother," she said, "I'm happy in my room. I can't imagine what silliness came over me!"

All the pieces of the puzzle fit now except one. What was the *reason* behind this powerful attempt to force us out of Zurich before our suitcases were even unpacked? Two months later we had our answer to that question, too.

Steve played basketball with local missionaries on their P day, and he invited several home to have his mother cut their hair. I was happy to do it, but we were dismayed to find that morale in the mission was low. Switzerland was a beautiful place to visit, but it was hard on young men trying to spread the gospel.

As I chatted with them one-on-one in the kitchen as wisps of hair fell onto the floor, it was obvious they were not sold on the value of what they were doing.

The Swiss people were self-sufficient, they complained, with no need or even inclination for religious instruction. The missionaries were wasting their time.

Also, that tiny country, extremely expensive for foreigners, was disastrous for missionaries on fixed incomes from home. Rents were shocking, and because of that their living quarters were more than humble, not conducive to building spirituality. Most of these fine young men were treading water, eager for the next two years to be over and done with.

While I had them alone in the kitchen I asked them individually what they would report when they spoke at sacrament meeting back home. Could they say these had been the best two years of their lives? They sadly shook their heads.

One Sunday night six missionaries knocked on our door with their usual complaints. Steve's own mission was approaching, and he had made up his mind that afternoon that, before he left, something positive had to be done.

Now he opened his Book of Mormon, found a particularly intriguing passage of scripture, and beckoned to the nearest elder. They drifted over to our small dining room table with its built-in seats. One by one, others were drawn in by the intensity of their discussion.

At the end of an hour they were elated. One sighed, "That was great! If we could meet here once a week and study together, I believe my whole attitude might change."

We watched it happen. The discouraged elders, it turned out, had much to give to each other in an informal setting. Their president was a spiritual giant, but constraints of his calling didn't allow for an extra night. He issued his blessing, so long as the gatherings didn't interfere with hours set aside for their work.

In no time, gloomy conversations between the Sunday night get-togethers turned from complaints to testimony-building experiences. The Swiss people were not so bad after all!

What Steve initiated continued long after he went to his own mission field in Germany. Every Sunday night, for as long as we lived in Zurich, two different elders chose a topic particularly dear to their hearts and spearheaded the discussion, while the others pored over open scriptures and eagerly joined in.

Sometimes we learned about ancient Coptic documents which corroborate our understanding of the gospel, taught brilliantly by Elders Ricks and Peterson, BYU students of ancient languages.

Once we vicariously lived through Indian adoption proceedings as a group member described his initiation into the Apache tribe at seven years of age in a formal ceremony in Colorado, a rite handed down from generation to generation and having striking points of similarity to our temple ceremony. Elder Brady spoke carefully so as not to breach the Apache chief's sacred trust.

Months passed away, transfers came and went, and occasionally transferred elders or sisters hopped on a train to come back to recharge their batteries. Once or twice twenty-four of us huddled three-deep around our table.

In the course of the discussions, exceptional young men and women reaffirmed to us and to each other that what they had been taught to believe is true.

They did it all themselves. We merely furnished the environment that made those glorious hours possible—and baked massive quantities of chocolate chip cookies!

Speaking for ourselves, we had truly unbelievable adventures all over Europe, but those Sunday evenings at Imbisbuhlstrasse Seben were times we will never forget.

What a coup for the adversary if he had snatched them away before they had a chance to begin!

11

The Process
of Passing

Marguerite Gibson had an unnatural fear of death. So much so that the patriarch who gave her her patriarchal blessing sensed her fear and addressed it. Her blessing stated that when death came she would welcome it as a friend.

We were roommates for two years in off-campus Gaisford House in Berkeley, California, and we grew very close in our little second-story room at the end of the hall, as roommates often do. We had long, intimate talks.

Perhaps Marguerite's dread of the unknown was not so much inborn as inherited, from her grandmother's fierce and lengthy struggle with the spectre of death, a struggle that was unnecessary, as it turned out, and in the final hour went easily and well.

We wondered together about the process of passing, and one late night as we lay on our beds waiting to fall asleep she told me her grandmother's story.

Margaret Lehman was Marguerite's mother. She was born and raised in Switzerland, in St. Gallen, a small town not far from the larger city of Zurich.

Surrounded by other countries, by other cultures with their own unique customs and languages, it isn't surprising that Swiss children are fluent in several tongues. Margaret and her sister, Lottie, spoke German, Swiss dialect, and English quite well and communicated fairly easily in Italian, Spanish, and a little French. Their familiarity with language is important later in this story.

The sisters were almost grown when their mother, Anna Maria Naef Lehman, moved them away from Switzerland. To put it as kindly as possible, her husband (the girls' father) was involved in a life-style she could no longer condone. The strength of her resolve was such that, with courage and only thirty dollars after the cost of transportation, she bustled them off to Utah to mingle with the Saints.

Margaret and Lottie earned another thirty dollars singing Swiss folksongs for first-class passengers on the ship.

Uprooting their lives to that extent *required* courage, because the mother didn't speak English. She found employment ironing in the Rowland Hall Girls' School in Salt Lake City, and the little family managed financially. Lottie took a quick refresher course in English and worked for the telephone company. In due time Margaret did the same.

Several years after their arrival in Utah, Margaret met the man she would ultimately marry. They met at an LDS function. He wasn't a member of her church, though he enjoyed attending its services. They quickly fell in love. Arvin and Marguerite were born to this happy union.

Marguerite's grandmother was a fine woman who did have extraordinary courage. She also had a will of iron, plus the old-country conviction that children owe everything to the parents who gave them life. Before the girls married she required that all the money they earned be turned over to her to manage, for the good of the family. Neither could date without taking their mother along. They were raised in this fashion and they had grown to accept it.

After Lottie married, Anna Maria moved into the newlyweds' home, and her possessiveness contributed to the breakup of the marriage. She didn't mean any harm. As a matter of fact, the honest and honorable woman didn't comprehend what she had done. She simply believed with her whole heart that her children owed her complete and eternal obedience, and in her mind their getting married changed nothing at all.

As small children, Arvin and Marguerite were uneasy with their grandmother's demands, and when visiting together as a family everybody felt the strain.

The grandmother grew older and developed a fatal lung disease. Her doctor shook his head and announced that her condition was undeniably serious. She could go at any time.

But the dying woman hung on—and on—and on.

"She's living by sheer will power," the doctor explained. "By every medical standard, she should be dead."

Still she refused to go. "I *won't* go—not without taking my girls with me," she repeatedly said. To those who knew her well, it was obvious that was exactly what she meant.

Three years passed, years of enormous suffering for the woman, but without the slightest relaxing of her resolve.

One night daughter Margaret woke with a start in her home in Willows, California. That was odd. What had awakened her? Glancing at the clock on the bedstand she noted that it was 2:30 A.M.

At the same moment she realized that something else was not normal. A man was in the house and he was speaking! She clearly heard the man's voice coming from the area of the living room, but strangely enough she wasn't frightened. Just the opposite. While she listened, spellbound, it didn't occur to her to question the sense of peace that filled the room.

Margaret concentrated on the words. What was the speaker saying? Familiar with so many languages, she listened for a recognizable root word. Not a syllable had she ever heard before.

The voice continued for perhaps ten minutes, the words caressing her ears with a quality not unlike the flowing of water. In her description to Marguerite later on, they resembled the splash of a waterfall as it skips and sings on its journey to the sea. Water is wonderfully restful, and so was the voice.

At last the words were stilled, and Margaret drifted comfortably back to sleep.

The next morning she woke to the ring of the telephone. Lottie was calling to tell her that their mother was gone. Anna Maria had slipped away in her sleep.

Margaret believed then that she knew exactly what she heard in the night. Sent to guide her mother back home, a loving and compassionate spirit had allowed her to stop by at Margaret's for one final good-by.

Margaret never lost her conviction that even in death her mother resisted the inevitable, and that Margaret herself had been privileged to witness the gentle persuasion—in the pure tongue of heaven—that convinced her mother to let go.

Marguerite passed away six years after that night when we spoke of death and dying. We lived in separate cities by then, and outside of an occasional planned meeting to bring each other up to date we had no opportunity for regular contact.

I didn't hear of her passing until several months after it occurred, and at the time I had few details. I thought about her patriarchal blessing. She interpreted the death-as-a-friend promise to mean that wars, famines, or global catastrophes would make life so unbearable that she would welcome release.

That hadn't been the case. I was puzzled.

Sometime later Marguerite's cousin Glenna moved to our ward, and she filled me in on the circumstances. Marguerite died of polio, tragically one of the last of its victims before Salk vaccine was available. Hers was the cruelest form of the cruel disease, and during her last six days she barely existed in an iron lung, paralyzed, not able to breathe on her own and without hope of recovery.

Living in the world, we are all subject to ailments of the flesh. Fortunately, a loving Father has prepared a way out.

I have no doubt that death came to Marguerite as a friend.

12

The True Believer

It's interesting to look backward and trace the formation of deep and abiding love.

A kinship exists automatically between Latter-day Saints who come together anywhere in the world. My husband, Ed, and I have traveled extensively in foreign countries and have welcomed that bond, that sense of the instant presence of love.

But one afternoon in Heidenheim, Germany, in March 1987, we became aware that spirituality in general—shared adoration for God and his Only Begotten Son—nourishes roots that reach out even beyond the boundaries of Church affiliation.

Sometimes shared adoration overturns old and bitter enmities and links the very souls of "true believers."

Karl Kohler seemed more thoughtful than usual that afternoon. Maybe it was because Ed and I were back in

Europe for what could be our last visit, at least for a while. The work that had taken my husband around the world many times over a period of years was almost finished.

We'd visited Herr Kohler in his office that morning, and now the three of us were lunching elegantly at a huge old twelfth-century fortress that sits atop a hill and dominates the picturesque city of Heidenheim.

As the luncheon progressed and we enjoyed delicious Wurst and Noodeln (and politely tolerated their Mineral Wasser), Karl touched briefly on basic differences in personality between Americans and Germans.

He expressed his view that Americans are more open. We make friends more easily, he said. But when a German finally offers his friendship, that friendship is for life.

We wondered where this unusual conversation was headed. Germans *are* formal. Colleagues work side by side for twenty-five years and rarely call each other by first names.

When Ed and Karl met for the first time on Ed's 1980 business trip to Europe, the two men were drawn to each other on sight. They look somewhat alike, both tall and lean, both handsome, with touches of gray sprinkled through their dark hair. They liked each other immediately, and probably because of our more casual American approach they uncharacteristically moved to a first-name basis rather quickly.

Nevertheless, during luncheon that day we were surprised when Karl gave tentative indications of acknowledging out loud how he felt about us. We reciprocated. From the intensity in his eyes, we sensed he spoke of emotions not easy for him to express.

"We are a private people," he began. "Nobody knows the real German man."

We waited, took another bite of the wonderful hard-crusted roll (eaten without butter in that part of the world), and then prompted, "You mean you have thoughts and feelings—fears, even—that you can't bring yourself to reveal?" Yes, he said, that was what he meant.

"But Ed, you are a true believer," he explained. We had suspected all along that Karl carried within himself some measure of faith in God. More than once when they were alone, Karl had asked Ed to explain some point of our doctrine, and Ed had gladly done so. There were no LDS branches, wards, or even missionaries in the area, so Ed presented Karl with a German-language edition of the Book of Mormon. The next time they met, Karl had read it through and enjoyed it.

Karl continued: "When true believers meet, a trust is born that goes beyond friendship. True believers recognize each other, as I recognized you."

Ed was touched. He responded in kind, but spoke sparingly. Neither of us wanted to risk breaking the mood. We thought there might be more Karl was determined to say.

He mused about his mother, who had always worshipped God. When Hitler came into power, she resisted giving him the adoration he required. She refused to go along with the Heil Hitler salute, a refusal punishable by death.

But his mother was fortunate to have loyal friends. Because they lived in a small outlying village where she was known and respected, she escaped punishment. Townspeople tolerated her eccentricity and protected her.

Karl was an impressionable teenager at the time. His mother urged him to put his trust in Jesus Christ, but he "knew better." "Mother, your God is somewhere way up there in the sky," he told her. "I can't see him. Hitler is here. Look what Hitler does for our people."

And at first that was true. Germans were starving, and Hitler provided them with jobs. He offered hope. He taught them to believe that as a nation, they were invincible.

Young Karl trusted Hitler completely. He worshipped his hero. All of his hopes and dreams for the future rested on his Fuhrer's shoulders, and he never once questioned whether his allegiance was properly placed.

When war broke out, Karl eagerly joined Hitler's army and fought for the brave new world he was convinced that, together, the fighting men of Germany would create.

The war raged on, and some years later Karl was in the midst of a ferocious battle. Men were falling all around him, and the young soldier was convinced that he, too, was in the last few moments of his life.

"All at once I saw my mother on her knees, praying for my safety," he said. "Don't ask me how it happened—I only know that I *saw* her, on her knees on that battlefield, and I *knew* at that moment that my life would be spared. I felt I could have risen up to walk safely through the hailstorm of bullets. That's how sure I was that because of my mother's prayers I would be spared."

The war was nearing an end when for the first time young Karl visited a Nazi concentration camp and witnessed for himself the carnage committed there. "I hadn't known—I swear I hadn't known!" he cried. Rumors had circulated, of course, but the young man's mind refused to consider even the possibility of such horrors.

Sickened beyond belief, he stared at the proof of his leader's insanity, and in that instant he was completely disillusioned. Everything he had believed in was brutally stripped away. By then Hitler was dead—by a coward's suicide—and now, for Karl, even the memory of the man's supposed greatness was gone. There was nothing in life left to cling to.

"Now, at last," he murmured, "I knew him for what he was."

German soldiers were captured by the thousands. Friends advised Karl not to let himself be taken by the Russians. "If you can manage it," they said, "put yourself in the hands of Americans."

And so he did. He was malnourished, since once again all of Germany was starving, and again he felt that death was his closest companion. What did it matter? He had nothing to live for anyway.

We interrupted at that point. This was the perfect opportunity to discover what life was really like for a German under the power of wartime American guards. I tried to make it easy for him to tell us the truth of the situation, good or bad.

I said, "Karl, I'm curious. How were you treated? During the war we in the United States feared and hated your country. We thought you were all monsters, without exception. A few years ago, I couldn't have imagined sitting at a table and lunching with a—a *German* (I believe I may have allowed myself to shudder at the thought), let alone to consider him a friend. You must have felt the same way about us."

"Actually," he said thoughtfully, "we were treated quite well, all things considered. Our unit insignia was a skull and crossbones, similar to the dreaded SS troopers. Before we were captured, we tore our insignias off. The SS were butchers, and we were terrified that we might be mistaken for them."

The strategy didn't work. Outlines of the round emblems were indented into the fabric of their shirts, and they *were* thrown in with the SS.

"The Americans hated us, but they didn't mistreat us," he said. "I understood their repulsion. I hated myself after seeing the horrors of Dachau."

Prisoners slept on open ground because of the enormous numbers taken captive so rapidly, and due to the shortage of food the first two weeks the men existed in near starvation. "That wasn't the fault of our guards," we were relieved to hear Karl say. "There simply wasn't food to be found."

There was more. "I was always taught that a Nazi never cries, no matter what. Yet all around me, broken men cringed and sobbed." If anything else were needed, now the young man's disillusionment with the once-proud Nazi life-style was complete.

Ill and despondent, he lay on the ground waiting for death. Then someone called his name. Raising his head weakly from the ground, he heard a guard call out "Karl Kohler! Karl Kohler!" He struggled to his feet.

The guard held out a good-sized package that had come in the mail, and it was addressed to him. How was that possible? Prisoners were known by numbers, not by names, even among the guards. Who could have sent it? He had been shuttled between four or five different camps, and nobody in the world who knew his name also knew where he might be located.

But there it was—Karl Kohler—written in big black letters on the brown wrapping paper covering the box.

Karl paused in his narrative and a look of sadness came over his face. He seemed determined to tell it all, to have us really understand.

He said, "That package was food—glorious food—and I'm sorry to tell you that in my starving condition I ate almost every bite of it myself. That food saved my life. I survived captivity and eventually was able to return to my home."

Ed quietly asked, "Where *did* the food come from?" Karl looked surprised. "It was sent from God, of course. He wanted me to live and he sent me food. There's no other answer that makes sense."

Back home again, Karl questioned his mother about the life-saving food. She, too, was puzzled. "Karl, you know we had no idea where you were being held. How could we have sent you anything?"

He thought back to his vision of her on the battlefield. "Mother, what were you doing on such-and-such a day? Were you praying for me?"

Her answer was, "I can't remember that day in particular, but never an hour went by that I didn't pray for your welfare. When you say you saw me, you can be sure that at that very moment I was indeed praying."

Karl accepted then that he had been the recipient of two miracles. Still, he found it difficult to offer absolute allegiance to anyone or anything for a second time. The wound from his first mistake was still too fresh, and the pain too deep. But over the span of years his trust in the Lord deepened until he became, as he now puts it, "a true believer."

Ed and I have never been more moved. This special man went against everything in his training and culture to reveal himself to us, flaws and all. We were deeply flattered; he trusted us to understand what, in its entirety, he might never have shared with another living soul.

During the war Karl and Ed fought on opposite sides, as dedicated, mortal enemies. Karl risked our disgust by admitting how freely he had embraced Hitler's philosophy in his youth.

He didn't bare his soul lightly, and we hadn't received his confidence without pain. Our eyes filled with tears several times during the two hours we lingered over lunch, and the bonding we felt became an eternal thing. We hesitated to end this time of special closeness.

We trudged back down the steep hillside, careful not to slip on remnants of snow along the muddy path. We came to the parting of our ways on a busy street corner. Karl must return to his office, and we would continue our half-work, half-pleasure odyssey through other parts of Europe.

Karl shook my hand, then kissed me gently on the cheek. That kiss surprised me. I wasn't used to the absence of aloofness that is so much a part of German life.

But it was for Ed that Karl reserved his deepest demonstration of affection and his sense of loss at their parting. He gripped Ed's hand, and looking deeply into his eyes, he whispered, "Ed, I will never forget you."

We hurried away in opposite directions, perhaps never again to meet in life, but with a spiritual love that will outlast time.

Ed said nothing at all—*could* say nothing for the next two blocks. But I knew he was pondering what mutual love for the Savior had overcome, and that in his heart he was repeating, "And Karl, my friend—my dear, dear friend—*I* will never forget *you!*"

13

The Banishment of God

In Russia in 1975 there was no perestroika. There was no glasnost, or open communication with the West. Many of the country's churches had been converted into museums of Atheism and Antiquities, and entire walls of once-holy cathedrals displayed their posters of war.

Officials were proud of these buildings and fostered the atheism they represented. Guides were baffled when outsiders visited the museums and cried.

On the surface it appeared to religiously inclined travelers that the Lord had been banished from Russian soil.

Donald and Nadine West joined a group of thirty-six for a bus tour of Russia in September 1975. Nadine was the only Mormon, but most of the others were Christians of various denominations. According to the Belgian guide, theirs may have been the first group to be allowed to tour that section of Russia—by bus—for many years.

As recently as the summer before, tourists had flown from city to city by plane, scheduled so as to arrive after dark and to leave in the dark. Strangers were not free to move about on their own. They saw only what was specifically approved for foreign eyes.

But it's hard for Americans to limit themselves in that fashion. Friendly and eager for contact with people, the Wests and their friends sometimes found themselves stopping to return a smile, or stepping through a hedge to watch as peasants harvested fall crops.

At first they didn't realize that towers they passed along the way were checkpoints, that their progress was being carefully monitored. When a picnic at the side of the road took a little too long, uniformed police from the tower ahead roared up on motorcycles, loaded machine guns in hand, to see for themselves why the bus hadn't checked in.

When the group looked forward to a free day, they were frustrated to hear, "With your free day, you will go to the circus."

Yes, Russia presented a different way of life, and by the time their bus pulled up at a motel on the outskirts of Smolensk travelers on board were beginning to chafe under the strain.

World War II was still very much in evidence. Smolensk had been occupied by the German army for two years back in the 'forties, and old bitterness at seeing their men and boys shipped to labor camps had never gone away. Women were left without men to till the fields, and most of the men didn't come home.

Citizens of Smolensk had just held a joyous celebration. Their numbers were decimated by the war, and it took until 1975, a full thirty years, for the population to match what it had been before the fighting began.

The area's church had been turned into an armory,

with a soldiers barracks next door, and except for those two structures the town had been virtually destroyed.

Priceless icons dating back hundreds of years had been removed by the populace and hidden away, kept safe, to be returned only after the enemy left. The people were so faithful in their belief in those days that they continued to go to the church, to stand outside, even after it was used to store arms.

It was late afternoon on a Saturday when the tour bus reached the motel in Smolensk. The rooms were grim and uninviting, so several of the group chatted outside in the open air. Farmers in the surrounding woods gathered mushrooms or colorful fall leaves.

Suddenly a local bus pulled up with a flurry of squealing brakes, and on impulse the Wests and three of the men jumped aboard. They wouldn't go far, but the opportunity to be on their own—if only for a few minutes—was too much to resist.

The bus was a big one, accordion-pleated in the middle, and it was packed with friendly, chattering people who were obviously curious about Americans. One man presented Nadine with an enormous apple. She smiled her appreciation and tucked the apple into her purse. Others followed suit until her purse brimmed over with apples. Whatever problems existed between heads of state, they didn't filter down to these passengers on the bus.

Drawing out pictures of her children, Nadine showed them all around. From time to time women in rough clothing reached out shyly to feel the fabric of her dress or to touch her curly hair.

Nadine enjoyed those few minutes, but much too soon the bus pulled into its terminal and the ride was over. She hadn't felt the least bit threatened or unsafe. In fact, she had been among friends.

Directly across the street an open-air market was just closing. Most of the stalls were already shuttered, so the five Americans turned to explore in the opposite direction.

Smolensk is a village-type town. They reached a cross-roads, and the other three, slightly ahead of the Wests, started down a street at random while Nadine paused to look at a plaque.

She couldn't make out the words, but she was filled with the strange and compelling notion that something important was about to happen. She had no idea where the path in front of her led; she only knew that that was the way she should go. As she hesitated, a man with a beret on his head stopped, smiled, and urged her along.

Nadine called to the others, and together they moved up the road that beckoned her.

It wasn't the easiest route they could have chosen. Lengthy stone staircases in four separate units, with flat ground in between, led them upwards, their ultimate destination hidden by a bend in the road.

Nadine didn't have a clue where they were going.

Halfway up the last set of stairs she became aware of singing. Not words and not loud, but clear, a kind of rejoicing sound, in unison, high and sweet, like the voices of children. She looked up, and having navigated most of the steps, now she could see where they were headed.

It was a church. Not the most beautiful building she had ever seen, but definitely a church. At the same time she noticed that she felt somewhat breathless.

She walked into a small courtyard dotted with wooden benches, where women were preparing themselves to enter the church. All wore old, soiled kerchiefs on their heads, which they now removed, replacing them with snowy white scarves with print at the edges. One small, weathered woman was dusting her wornout shoes with a rag.

These were elderly peasants, not women of the world, but observing their actions Nadine was strangely touched.

She felt uncomfortable in their presence, as if she should not invade their sacred and private place.

All the women were beaming at her, however, as if to say, "Go ahead. Please go in." To show respect for their customs, she pulled a scarf out of her purse and tied it under her chin. Then she stepped across the threshold.

The room was fairly small and was dimly lit. There were no pews, no places to sit. The windows were deep set and narrow, and the icons were so old that they had turned black.

At the time she didn't notice the huge fireplace on one wall—didn't consciously process much of anything, except for the shock of the spirit that permeated the church, a force so intense that it was painful. The awesome presence of God struck her so forcibly that she became faint.

She knew she was on hallowed ground. She felt as she imagined one would feel in the celestial kingdom if not entirely worthy to be there. Sudden tears streamed down her cheeks. She trembled violently and knew she had to sit down.

Weakly she groped her way to the courtyard and dropped down on one of the wooden benches. Her husband hurried after her and, puzzled, took her in her arms. She desperately wanted to go back in, but she couldn't.

The next day she was determined to go back. She was amazed that the church had survived the war and that she had been lucky enough to find it.

The singing confused her. Searching her memory she was positive she hadn't seen a choir or a choir loft, and she couldn't call up the picture of a separate room. Where could the owners of those voices have been? She had to go back to find them.

The church wasn't on their day's schedule, but when Nadine pressed her the guide agreed to take them there.

Nadine steeled herself to the onslaught of emotion that she knew awaited her, and this time she was better prepared. All she could think of was how much she desired to go back. With the support of all the other Christians on the tour, hopefully this time she would not be totally overcome and could remain inside a little longer.

Where there had been older worshippers on Saturday, on Sunday entire families were climbing the hill to the church. Some were dressed more fashionably than those on the previous day. Some were not. Some carried canes and took a long time mounting the stairs. An especially elderly woman started up slowly when they did, and as they left she was barely reaching the top.

Again the singing greeted them halfway up the last flight of stairs, although when Nadine searched the chapel she couldn't locate the singers. There were no other rooms. Even the area where the priest prepared his sacrament was flung wide open that day. She never did discover the source of the music.

The music had sounded as clear outside as it did now that she was inside. The hearth on the fireplace held offerings of vegetables from the gardens of the people. Stepping to the middle of the room, she folded her hands, bowed her head, and said a silent prayer. She was prepared, and this time she could drink in the spirit.

Opening her eyes, she noticed a pair of men's shoes on the floor three feet in front of her, shoes that were clean, polished, and very, very old. The feet and ankles in them were much too small for the shoes and they were bare of stockings. Nadine's gaze rose to a man's worn coat draping below the occupant's thighs. She couldn't see the hands; they were covered by the sleeves.

Finally her eyes reached the head of the individual who wore the men's clothes, and she wasn't even five feet tall. Again Nadine was humbled to the point of tears she couldn't control. The look on that woman's sweet face was the epitome of peace. So serene; so secure. What most of humanity searches for in vain, she had already found.

Nadine's thought was, "When I see that woman's face up in heaven, I will know her."

She was so overcome that she barely made it out of the door and onto a bench. Was she the only one to be thus affected by this place? She looked around, through her tears. No, other members of her group were openly crying.

Two Russian grandmothers, big and robust, came to her side and pressed in closely. Nadine sensed a sisterhood as the three of them comforted each other and silently confirmed that, after everything these fine people had been through, including wars and the purge of religion, in spite of existing under a godless regime, nothing could kill the belief that sustained them.

Now there *is* glasnost and perestroika, and the churches of the country have been reopened.

Had God really been banished for a time from Russian soil? Not from a little pocket of the faithful on a hilltop near Smolensk.

14

Nadia of the East

How did she *ever* get into this position?

How could she get out?

Susan pondered her options while she pulled on the long black garment that by law she was forced to wear when she stepped beyond the doors of the mini-palace she now called home.

Admittedly, she lived in fairy-tale luxury, like a princess out of the Arabian Nights. The chauffeur-driven Jaguar stood by to whisk her to her destination, but always it was a destination she had no opportunity to choose for herself.

She lived in luxury but also in fear, a prisoner in a golden cage from which there was no escape, a captive whose precious identity was being literally stripped away.

But she *must* escape! Her mind darted as she arranged the veil over her face so that the only part of her anatomy a stranger could see was her eyes.

No! She couldn't live this way forever. She wouldn't! Even with no one to turn to for help, there had to be a way out—and if she died in the attempt, she would find it!

Susan was a widow and no doubt vulnerable when she met Randy*—a blond, blue-eyed physician and the most charismatic man she had ever encountered. He was a six-year convert to The Church of Jesus Christ of Latter-day Saints.

Before they married she knew, generally, that he had a problem with the Internal Revenue Service over back, unpaid taxes, but when she broached the subject more specifically with Randy or his accountants they were vague in their responses.

He mentioned a past divorce. The marriage hadn't worked out, he said, and the separation hadn't been amicable. But that was prior to his conversion to the Lord, while he was still an atheist with totally different family standards. Any problems in that direction were surely behind him now.

Susan's twenty-five-year marriage to her grown children's father had been a good one, so she wasn't prepared for anything less.

Randy was highly respected in his field. Susan was proud of him. He was considered one of the most expert emergency doctors anywhere, and he had written a number of widely-used medical manuals. He lived well in an incredibly huge and beautiful home.

Susan herself operated a lucrative family-marriage-and-child-counseling service in the city where they'd met, so she went into the marriage with every confidence of success. Both made good money and both were intelligent; they would work out his financial hangups together.

---

*The names have been changed, but the facts are true.

After the wedding she was shocked to learn the extent of Randy's tax problem. Her husband had seriously misrepresented his financial situation. He'd made millions of dollars but, strangely, had gone through bankruptcy proceedings—twice—and hadn't paid a cent to the government for years. Now the IRS was prepared to confiscate the house and everything he owned and to put a lien on future earnings, leaving him only three hundred dollars a month to live on.

Susan discovered something else about her husband. Randy was definitely not a man to be put in a box. He liked to win. He couldn't tolerate *anyone* telling him what he could or couldn't do. Outwitting the agency that was determined he should pay what he rightfully owed became a kind of game to Randy. It was invigorating! And there were viable options he planned to pursue.

He could take his bride out of the country for a time. Not for long—certainly not forever. Only until they made arrangements to square his account with the government. To the basically trusting Susan that approach sounded like a good idea, at the time.

He'd located a firm which arranged international placement for doctors who wanted to travel. That was their business. Company executives suggested it might be well for Randy to look into Saudi Arabia. The corporation had a work agreement between the United States and the royal hospital in Riyadh, the capital city. Doctors in Arabia were paid fabulous salaries and were looked upon by the people virtually as gods.

Yes, the trip would be like stepping onto another planet —an adventure straight out of an Arabian Nights fairytale!

The way it worked, they were advised, was that physicians practice in Arabia on a *locum* or trial period. The contract stated that at the end of two months they must return to the United States, with a choice of going back again if they so desired. Set up for such a short period, the move appealed to Susan as a rare and fascinating opportunity.

But first there were volumes of paper work to be completed. Tourism, as such, is non-existent in Arabia. Nobody steps casually onto a plane and flies to that country without proper visas and, more important, without some specific purpose. Waiting for official permission, Randy took Susan to the South Pacific for three months, where he filled the slot of a doctor who was on extended leave. Those months away from home turned out to be sheer heaven, and a welcome rest from turmoil over finances. Both had a wonderful time.

Then they were called back to the United States, where the paperwork had been completed and visas put in order, and a plane—with Randy and Susan packed, excited, and on it—lifted gracefully into the air early in 1988. Their adventure had begun.

Right from the beginning, it appeared that Randy had found his niche. In two weeks he was appointed head of an entire section of the hospital. In that melting pot of brilliant medical minds from all over the world, he was again a standout.

Contact was made with the Church, and Susan was allowed to come and go to the extent that women can come and go in a country where wives have no legal rights at all and husbands hold total control over their family's lives. She made friends inside of church and out, and even worked part-time at the hospital emergency room, under her husband's direction.

But she felt considerable stress. Women in Arabia live under restriction. She had known that, but reality exceeded her imagination. Restriction was considered protection, freeing women from the necessity of making decisions.

Western women were not respected there, and to Susan

that was a frightening and demeaning thought. The freedom she'd taken for granted in the United States was suddenly gone without a trace. She and Randy lived in a compound set aside for doctors, a palace surrounded by forbidding walls. Guards at the gate twenty-four hours a day refused to let her leave the compound—even in her chauffeur-driven car—without her husband's express permission.

Some months earlier King Fahd had visited the United States as a guest of President Ronald Reagan and toured the medical facility at the White House. Back home, he wanted that care for himself and his extended family—emergency room specialists at his beck and call without having to leave the palace.

In his position as head of the general hospital emergency room, Randy was charged with training the palace physicians. As a result (and with natural charisma), he grew extremely close to the royal family and very shortly found himself the possessor of enormous power. Susan noticed with alarm how he thrived on that heady sense of power.

Almost every morning the king's limousine glided to their door to pick him up, transporting him into a world of unbelievable wealth and indulgences. In no time he fit into that opulence as naturally as a duck slips into the water he is born to.

The king loved him. In another two weeks, Randy managed to circumvent the hard-and-fast rule of returning to the States after the two-month trial period. Somehow he talked his way into permanent resident status, and without one word of input being requested from his wife it was made official.

From time to time Randy praised the strength of the Muslim religion, which in itself was not frightening. Susan learned to admire the tenets of Muslim faith, their stated love for peace, their strong family ties. Randy studied the Koran and his wife didn't object. It was a beautiful document. Susan read a portion of it herself.

She admired the Muslim devotion to their beliefs as a people and respected their total dedication. Five times a day the call to worship sounds from minarets sprinkled liberally on the streets, and the entire country stops, washes the body, prays, then washes again. No division at all exists between powers of church and state.

Women are enjoined from praying in public. Every store or gas station has a private prayer room available. The men, however, seek out companionship, believing that for them there is power in united prayer.

But more ominous were Randy's comments concerning taking other wives, a legal and almost universal practice in that country so frighteningly far from home. One day Susan ran across papers in the desk proving he had gone so far as to inquire into purchasing a wife from Asia. When she confronted her husband, he laughed. It was a joke! Nothing more.

Friday is the day set aside for Sabbath worship in Arabia, and Latter-day Saints—who are a tiny minority, of course—seek to follow custom as much as possible and so observe that day as *their* Sabbath. More and more often, Randy worked on Fridays. Susan couldn't dismiss the suspicion that his schedule was deliberately conceived. Working gave him an excuse not to attend the Mormon church.

Then he stopped calling her Susan. She became his *Nadia of the East.*

Muslim law dictated that every time she left the house she must dress in the typical long black *gandoura* that hides the body, but infidels are not compelled by law to wear a veil to hide the face. Randy found the mystery of the veil intriguing and insisted that Susan make use of that covering fabric.

Little by little, before her horrified eyes, the husband she had trusted underwent a terrible metamorphosis. He changed into a monster she didn't know or love, as surely as kindly Dr. Jekyll had transformed into the terrifying Mr. Hyde. Worse yet, this stranger held the legal power of life and death over her present existence and, if she didn't get away from him, over all the years of her future.

He exhibited fits of paranoid temper when she expressed an opinion. Once, out of control, he screamed, "You'll never get away from me. Never! Don't even try!"

To emphasize his dominance, he handed her a packet of letters. Her letters. Letters she had mailed from the hospital to family back home. Letters he had intercepted. For the first time, she comprehended the extent of his power.

Now, when it was too late, she appreciated the freedom of the United States with an almost religious fervor. She thought of her family so far away, of her children, and of her father who wasn't well. Would she ever see them again? Her mind searched in panic for a way to escape.

She trusted her friends at church but knew she couldn't involve them in her dilemma. Religions other than Muslim are tolerated in Arabia, at best. Proselyting by other faiths is prohibited and their legal influence is nil. No more than fifteen members of an organization may meet together at any one time. The merest hint that the bishop or his counselors had offered her assistance against her husband's wishes would cause problems for the Church in that land.

The day Randy informed her of his permanent resident status he magnanimously assured her she could go home for the summer to visit her children and parents. Susan quietly laid her plans, carefully concealing her fear that he might renege on the promise. Realizing her intentions, Randy announced that she couldn't go after all, and passed off the denial by saying it would spoil the treat he had thoughtfully arranged for her pleasure.

Two of her children—Lisa, twenty-seven, and Mike, twenty-two—were coming to visit her! Also, his son Sean, twenty, would join them for a month. What a rare opportunity for the children to experience in person what they might never in their lifetimes have another chance to savor!

Susan *was* delighted to see her children. She had no qualms that Randy would restrain them when the visit was over. In fact, it wasn't long before the effort of behaving like the man they used to know began to tell on him, and she sensed that he grew eager to see them go. All three were puzzled. Randy's son asked Susan over and over, "What's happened to Dad?" She didn't dare to tell him.

Before they arrived, Susan developed a habit of walking every evening. Exercise cleared her mind and gave her time to think. She was restricted to walking in the compound, but it helped. Her faith in the goodness of God, always strong, sustained her in her hours of hopelessness.

One day she stepped behind an outcropping of rocks where she could kneel without being observed. With all the fervor of her being she prayed to be delivered, and a cloud of protection seemed to envelop her soul. It was as if she received a promise that her hour of deliverance would come, and somehow she knew that this was a promise she could trust.

Beginnings of a vague plan took shape in her mind. Bahrain is a small independent territory adjoining Arabia, formerly having a British-protected status and still employing British guards at the border. Randy had taken her there once, a three-hour drive along a beautiful freeway. The gateway to Bahrain was a spot he might want to share with his guests.

The borders of Arabia and Bahrain stand there side by side. If she could arrange to get him close, could leap from the car, flee through the Arabian gate and onto Bahrain soil before anyone could stop her, surely the British guards would grant her asylum.

Susan was careful not to hint of her plans to the children. She couldn't risk letting an inadvertent word or expression in the eyes give it away. She continued to watch, and wait, and trusted that when the time came she could yell "Run!" and her son and daughter would follow her without question. Apparently Randy was lulled into believing she was content for the moment. He relaxed his guard.

Events played into her hands. The family celebrated Sean's twenty-first birthday at the Persian Gulf. On the way home, perhaps they could show Sean the marvelous structures on the Bahrain causeway. Randy agreed. He pulled to a stop by the border and Susan's heart beat faster when Sean noticed a huge poster he wanted as a backdrop for a snapshot. Laughing, the three young people climbed out of the car.

Out of the corner of her eye Susan glanced at the border and gauged its distance. Ever so casually she reached for the door handle, but before she could push the door ajar, Randy's hand shot out like a bullet propelled from a gun. His fingers gripped her arm so tightly that bruises remained as evidence the following day.

"Where do you think *you're* going?" he sneered. "Do you think I'm an idiot? I've already told you—you belong to me. You'll never get away!"

In spite of her protestations of innocence, his grip didn't loosen until Mike, Lisa, and Sean finished taking pictures and settled back into the car.

From that point on, Susan was really afraid. Sean and Mike eventually left for home. The hardest thing Mike had ever done was to leave his mother, sensing that something was wrong, but his visa was due to expire. He had no choice. Lisa would leave the country shortly.

Sometimes casual acquaintances understand far better than we think they do. An older doctor from Australia spoke to Susan at the hospital. "I've watched the changes in your husband and I understand your problem better than you suppose. Isn't there something you can hold against him as a threat?"

There was. Now Randy was abusing drugs. She located prescriptions on which he had forged her name, and she knew that in spite of his position of status with the king, drug use made public would destroy him. She confronted him: He would either arrange for her exit visa immediately and return her passport or she would report his illegal habit to the head of the hospital.

She emphasized that she didn't want anything material from him. She would leave with only the clothes on her back.

Randy went through all the motions. He tried to mask his outrage. Within two days her papers were in order, as were her daughter's, and their flight arrangements were made, but not for a second did Susan think he would let her go.

Granting permission to use the car to drive to the airport—or not—was still his privilege, and when the time arrived he would find some way to withhold it. On the surface she had won, but not really.

She prayed constantly; it was her only resource.

A young couple surprisingly risked coming to her rescue. By this time many sensed Susan's unhappiness. Randy didn't understand her friendship with the pair, so hopefully he wouldn't suspect their complicity. If she ever decided to leave, she was welcome to hide out with them for two days and nights, disappearing from the hospital before he expected her to make a move. The couple's car and driver were available if she needed them.

She accepted their generous offer but wouldn't allow them to travel the road with her.

The airport was miles from the city, and it was a beautiful building. Her friends' limo eased down the half-mile driveway—and out of all the acres of spaces to park, the driver pulled up right next to Randy's empty car. At sight of the vehicle, Susan was paralyzed with fear. She had pinned her hopes on the airport being a public place. Surely Randy wouldn't dare accost her there.

With eyes straight ahead she hurried Lisa through the enormous lobby. If they could get through customs they would be safe. Nobody is allowed past that point without a valid ticket.

But Lisa was stopped while going through the X-ray device. A technicality of some sort. They still don't know exactly why. Susan agonized until the difficulty was solved, and the two trembling women passed through. Now it was just a matter of staying calm until they boarded the plane.

Susan was standing next to the agent's counter with her back to the door when she *felt* Randy's approach. Fighting hysteria, she took a deep breath and turned to face him.

He took hold of her arm in another grip of iron and through clenched teeth he hissed, "I want to talk to you, Susan. As your husband I *demand* to know where you have been the past two days. Who helped you with this? Come outside so we can talk!"

Randy appeared not to have slept for several days. He was disheveled. He said, "If you won't come out with me, you *know* I can force you."

Susan stood very still, letting him rant. A second protecting cloud seemed to surround her, as it had the day she'd prayed behind the rocks.

At length Randy must have accepted that his power over her was gone. To *make* her leave would mean a public disturbance, and his ego would not allow it. His arm dropped, and in a loud voice he proclaimed, "Very well! I divorce you; I divorce you; I divorce you." This affirmation is the equivalent of divorce in Arabia.

Without another word he turned on his heel and strode out of her sight.

Susan reached America in September, and she literally dropped to the ground and kissed it. In October Randy showed up at the doors of each of her children. Back to his old charm, he tried in every way possible to convince them to reveal her whereabouts, but of course they didn't.

Later she learned that he stopped on the way back to Arabia to buy a twenty-six-year-old Asian woman, and that he has since considered marrying a Muslim also.

Marrying a Muslim in a Muslim country connotes complete conversion to that faith.

Will Susan ever lose her fear that one day she will look over her shoulder and Randy will be there? Probably not, emotionally, but intellectually she doesn't expect him to return. The IRS allowed him into the country in October because he agreed to meet with them to settle his account. When he didn't show, they were livid. He would be hard pressed to gain entry safely a second time on the same pretext.

Susan has started a new life now, grateful in the knowledge that when she found herself helpless, a stranger in a strange land, she nevertheless was not really alone.

15

Move!

It was an ordinary mid-January day on the channel between Vallejo, California, and Mare Island Naval Shipyard.

Large ferries transported huge numbers of workers to their jobs at the submarine building-and-launching base on the island, and marine guards were on hand to check identification papers before anyone boarded the boats. The year was 1943—wartime—and security around the base was tight.

Maybe there was a difference. Maybe the wind was a little colder and more blustery that day than usual. But then again, maybe not. Hack Severson couldn't tell. Winds whipping across this northern section of San Francisco Bay are always icy in the winter. Marine personnel and civilian employees waiting in a long line for the next ferry, lunchboxes in hand, were chilled to the bone.

That cold wind was the reason why sympathetic guards periodically relented and broke their hard-and-fast rule that *nobody* except marines could enter the guard shack on the pier. Teenage boys collected ferry tickets before and after school or rode back and forth across the channel as deck hands, and they were almost always half-frozen. The shack was warm. Permitting the boys to slip in occasionally to ease the chill had become routine procedure.

But this day started out like any other. As usual Hack, thirteen, dragged his resisting body out of its cozy bed at 5:30 A.M. Because of the war, workers, even young ones, were in great demand, and Hack's pay was an impressive thirty-five cents per hour. The Severson family wasn't well-to-do, and the youngster wanted to bring in all the money he possibly could.

He pumped his bicycle to Georgia Street, then took a boat down to the Vallejo side of the Rider Street dock and worked there for a couple of hours before pedaling off to class. Students with work permits were excused from school just before the last period of the day, so Hack was back at the dock and shivering by mid-afternoon.

Because tides on the bay constantly flow in and out, the ramp leading to the ferry was a long one, and shaped like an L. The covered guard shack located at the turn of that L was glass-enclosed on two sides. A sturdy four-by-four post held the glass walls together at the juncture.

The entire ramp rose and fell and shifted with the tides, and below the shack, moving water made a soft swishing sound. A desk and chairs were available inside for marines coming off duty and others waiting to take their places.

Guards weren't supposed to let anyone inside, but with the passage of time they had come to trust their "kids" and feel sorry for them.

Hack was warming up in the shack at 3:30 P.M., at the changing of the guards. He watched as two men in uniform came in and began the familiar ritual of taking off gun belts and slipping .45 calibre semi-automatics out of their holsters.

He'd seen that routine hundreds of times, and it was always the same: clip removed; slide pulled back to eject bullet from chamber; slide pulled back a second time to visually check that bullet had, in fact, left the chamber; gun pointed toward canvas ceiling; trigger squeezed as final confirmation that chamber was empty.

He'd noticed several holes in the overhead canvas, and they silently attested to the fact that nothing put together by man works perfectly 100 percent of the time. But in all the months he'd watched the ritual, nothing had gone awry. The guards on duty were seasoned veterans. Most had served overseas. They knew what they were doing.

However, this time one of the marines handling his gun was talking to a buddy, and his mind was evidently on something else. Maybe he did remove the clip. Maybe he did pull back on the slide, and with that one chance in a million the bullet didn't eject. But clearly he left out at least one crucial step: he neglected to point the barrel toward the ceiling before pulling the trigger.

Hack was six feet away, half leaning, half sitting on the edge of the desk.

Suddenly the boy heard a clear voice say distinctly, "Move." He was startled and confused. Immediately the voice came again, more firmly this time: "Move!" And precisely at that moment it was as if someone picked him up bodily and slid him two or three inches to the right. As he shifted, he heard the deafening roar of a shell exploding from the pistol. In the confines of the enclosed room, it was louder than he would have imagined possible.

The shack came alive! Every man in the room—including the startled teenager—leaped to his feet like puppets lifted by a single string. In two great strides, Sgt. Anderson reached the offending guard and sternly placed him under arrest.

Everybody else searched for the bullet. Where was it? No sign of broken glass from the two walls of windows. Forty-fives are big, blunt instruments capable of great destruction. Where had the murderous bullet lodged?

In a cluster they ran toward the wooden post. The shell that wasn't supposed to be in the chamber at all had torn its way completely through the heavy beam. It went in cleanly but came out leaving a gaping hole on the other side, typical procedure for a Colt .45.

Most of the guards raced outside, where the long line of ferry patrons stood in shock. One man was especially stunned. After clearing the post, the partially spent slug had blasted a hole in the worker's lunch box and had come to rest in the middle of his roast beef sandwich.

Hack was as curious about the accident as any of the adults. Eventually the excitement settled, and one of the marines remembered Hack and thought about where he had been. Startled, he yelled, "Hey, kid, weren't you leaning against the desk? You were right in the bullet's path. How come it didn't hit you?"

The guard moved closer as he spoke and pulled at the edge of Hack's jacket—brown leather on the front and sleeves, green knit on the back, with a red plaid lining. "What's this hole under the arm of your coat?"

Hack didn't remember a hole. His clothes *were* a bit threadbare because money was scarce, but they hadn't been falling apart. His eyes followed the man's pointing finger, and to his astonishment there really was a hole.

The guard helped the boy yank off his jacket. Closer examination disclosed a second hole under the sleeve.

With the jacket off, they looked at his shirt. Holes there, too, as if some intruding foreign object had forced its way in and then back out. Hack tore off his shirt, and by this time his heart was beating double-time.

His undershirt, the clinging kind with straps over the shoulder, with fit almost like a second skin, had *three* ragged bullet-sized tears.

Now it was obvious which pathway the bullet had chosen. Sitting directly between the gun's muzzle and the wooden post, Hack's body had been the perfect target. The shell had whistled between Hack's ribs and his left arm in a space that was practically nonexistent, moving so precisely that the boy hadn't felt so much as a draft.

What if Hack hadn't moved? The bullet, so powerful that it tore a gaping hole through a solid wooden post, would have made mincemeat of his chest.

What if his body had moved to the left instead of to the right? It would have blasted him squarely through the heart.

What if he had moved even half an inch farther to the right? The slug would have torn his arm off.

But he had moved—been moved—exactly the right distance, down to a fraction of a millimeter, and the bullet had slipped between his arm and his body so cleanly that he hadn't been aware of its passing.

From then on Hack was called "the miracle kid" far and wide. He saved the jacket and undershirt and has treasured them for more than forty years. My husband and I held them both in our hands. Our fingers explored the holes, and we marveled.

Was saving a young boy's life the only consideration that day? No. Hack Severson was our bishop when we lived in Rancho Cordova. He went on to become a counselor in the stake presidency, and for six years now has been a counselor to the president of the California Sacramento Mission. Who can say how many lives he has influenced for good since that day?

Experts on near death claim that what is experienced by the spirit is never forgotten. Hack remembers every detail of that should-have-been-fatal afternoon as clearly as if it were yesterday. He sees the long line of people winding their way down the ramp. He hears the soft swish of water and feels movement of the floor beneath his feet.

Most clearly of all, he hears the commanding voice ring out its warning.

"The miracle kid," needless to say, is still a strong advocate of heeding the promptings of the Spirit—without question.

16

Words of Conclusion

In the ten years I've researched and written true human interest stories of courage, conviction, or love, I've had some experiences and reached a conclusion or two that may be worthy to be shared.

Right from the beginning I determined to write accurately. If I stated a story was true, that was what I intended it to be, every whit. If a car featured in the plot even briefly, I planned to label the car blue, or red, or green, or whatever color it was in real life.

When I put together *The Crisis Room* for my book *No Greater Love*, the last thing in the world I expected was that *Reader's Digest* would see it, like it, and ask to reprint it. I wasn't aware that they employ a research team to check and double-check each word, nor that if one small error is uncovered the story is dropped.

A joke with one line of informational wit sends them anywhere in the world to verify the facts.

Every individual who was at the Suicide Prevention Agency on that fateful night when I helped to save a frantic young man in what would have been the last moments of his life was contacted by *Reader's Digest* and questioned in detail. Did the incident really take place? Was it *exactly* as the author claimed it to be? Five other agencies throughout the country were quizzed to be certain the flavor of a suicide hotline was identical to the way I portrayed it.

When I wrote *Three Inches From Life* as a combination Drama in Real Life for the *Digest* and chapter 3 of *In Loving Hands*, careful adherence to the truth had become second nature. Nevertheless, I breathed a sigh of relief when that story too survived the *Digest* acid bath of scrutiny and researchers issued their official stamp of approval. I felt my words had truly gone through the refiner's fire and not been found lacking.

How embarrassing it would have been to be caught in a fabrication—by experts! How grateful I was that I had not exaggerated, or added a detail here and there purely for dramatic effect!

When I record spiritual events, or out-and-out miracles, as several chapters of my books do, I feel strongly that each must contain some element that can be touched or handled, and verified. Or a life must change to the extent that coincidence is impossible.

For example:

It was 1981. My first book was all but finished when I received a call from our son Steven Seither, from Roswell, Georgia. His voice exuded excitement when he said, "Mother! Have I got a story for you!"

The report was that a counselor in the stake presidency there had just used his priesthood authority to call a member back from the dead—in full view of two hundred witnesses, including trained medical personnel who insisted that the man had been totally and undeniably gone.

Working in conjunction with the Spirit, in a sacred meeting to dedicate an empty lot for a proposed new chapel, the counselor called on the power of God to alter to a miraculous outpouring of God's love what otherwise would have remained a tragic memory forever. Now whenever those two hundred people worshipped at the site, they would remember the day they took part in a miracle.

That was my kind of story.

As luck would have it, I planned to visit Steve and Melanie within the week. My bags were packed and the airplane ticket was tucked away in my purse. A second baby was due to appear and, as mothers do, I had offered my help. I thanked Steve for calling and told him I would interview all parties concerned after I got there. I might have enough stories to fill the first book, but if all went well this story could be included in a second.

The baby arrived on schedule, and so did I. I washed and folded diapers for ten days without an opportunity to pursue my investigation, and then it was Sunday again and this time we were able to go to church.

We all went our separate ways after entering the foyer of a typical, beautifully appointed ward building. We were early, giving Steve a minute to check seating arrangements for his Gospel Doctrine class, and Melanie stepped into the restroom to change baby Justin.

I wandered into the chapel. It was empty except for four or five people busy with Sunday chores—setting up the sacrament table or testing the microphones to see that they worked.

One man didn't seem to have an assignment. He stood on the other side of the chapel. When he saw me he virtually ran down the aisle—and behind the middle rows of pews and back up the other aisle to where I stood—his hand stretched out to greet me.

He introduced himself as Max Kimball and asked me why I was there. I told him my name, that I was Steve Seither's mother, and that I had flown in from California to help with the new baby. That explanation didn't satisfy him.

Still gripping my hand and fixing me with a stare so intense that I began to feel uneasy, he insisted, "Yes, but why are you really here? Why else did you come?"

I assured him that my purpose *was* what I had explained. Then I excused myself and went to look for my son.

Sacrament meeting came first on the schedule in Roswell, and we gathered the family together on the third row of the chapel. Before the opening prayer, Steve tapped me on the shoulder and whispered, "See the man sitting on the stand? That's President Kimball. He's the one who called Brother Robinson back from the dead."

I looked where he pointed, and to my amazement President Kimball was Max Kimball, the man who had hurried across the chapel to ask me over and over what my real purpose was in coming.

Ward conference was in session that day. Brother Kimball was a visitor from the stake and, as it turned out, didn't even know Steve by name, because the Seithers were new to the area.

After the meeting was over, I sought *him* out. I explained that I was a beginning writer, hard at work on a book of faith-promoting true experiences. I planned to speak to other principals connected with Richard Robinson's remarkable journey back from the beyond—his daughter Barbara; missionaries standing by his elbow at the time of the massive heart attack; the nurse from the cardiac care unit of a local hospital plus the Australian ambulance attendant on the scene, who both administered mouth-to-mouth resuscitation and heart massage—and since Brother Kimball was undoubtedly a busy man, I would talk to him last and briefly. I would call him before I left for home.

The interviews went well. I was impressed with the power of statements from the medical people, how evident it is when a spirit leaves a body, and how there was no doubt that Brother Robinson was dead.

Recurring goose pimples ran up and down my spine when every person I questioned described an unnatural stillness in the air as President Kimball spoke in a voice that rang like thunder to listening ears, and commanded Richard Robinson's spirit to return to his body.

It was Tuesday afternoon when I called Brother Kimball, the last full day of my visit. He related his feelings and thoughts on the matter, and just before hanging up I thanked him for his time. I felt a bit apologetic, because I wasn't certain my book would be published. My editor had worked with me every step of the way and was hopeful, but she reminded me frequently that publication is never a certainty until every last word is complete.

I said, "I'm not *positive* my book will be published, but I think it has a good chance."

My blood chilled in my veins as President Kimball replied, "Oh, it will be published, Sister Mackay. Don't worry about that for a second. I knew the minute I saw you come into the chapel that you were on an errand for the Lord. The only thing I didn't know was what that errand was. That's why I questioned you about your purpose in coming."

He went on to state his belief that miracles have occurred since the world began, and that it is important for us as children of God to know they still happen today. But such stories are sacred, he cautioned. They must be handled sensitively or not at all. If I hadn't been the right person, if he hadn't known that I was, he wouldn't have agreed to the interview. He added, "I simply would have told you I don't have the information you need."

I hung the telephone on its hook on the kitchen wall, and by this time I was shaking uncontrollably. Melanie turned from the sink, alarmed. She said, "Mom, you are as white as a sheet. You look as if you might faint. What did he say to you?"

How should I reply? President Kimball hadn't said anything to warrant this type of reaction. He'd assured me that in his opinion my book would be published, and again, in his opinion, what I'd worked so diligently to accomplish was favored by the Lord. Wonderful words! Awe-inspiring thoughts! But mortal opinions, nonetheless.

I'm sorry to admit I don't have a history of *being able* to approach the Lord for direction and, as a result, know instantly what he desires of me. That isn't my talent, although I strive for it consistently.

I envy the fortunate few who describe how they beseech the Lord for promptings of the Spirit, receive a powerful answer, and conduct their lives accordingly. Almost always I agonize at life's crossroads, seldom knowing with assurance whether the decision I make comes through valid inspiration or is mine alone, based on the wishes of my heart.

In describing the telephone conversation to Steve minutes later, I commented wistfully, "Wouldn't it be *something* if President Kimball is right, if the Lord is mindful of my efforts?" The thought was almost too much to contemplate.

Steve took me sternly to task. "Mother," he said, "a spiritual giant close enough to his Father to call a man back from the dead has testified you are receiving guidance in your work. Your trembling is the Spirit confirming that he speaks the truth. How do you *dare* to doubt?"

But I did doubt. I couldn't help it. It wasn't until the finished book lay in my hands that I could admit to myself that President Kimball might—just might—have been right. And looking back, I see now that unwittingly I chose the very paths that led to this point, as surely as if I were following a blueprint some kindly draftsman laid out with great care.

This humbling incident is shared not to set myself apart, but as one more voice, another testimony that the Lord is mindful of all his children and that he daily influences our lives—even in those lonely moments when we don't feel his concern.

Another point to ponder:

Why do miracles occur in the lives of some of us and not others? Several chapters in my books document the return of loved ones from beyond the veil, intervention at crucial moments, or lives saved in a miraculous manner. Does this have to do with our state of righteousness? I think not.

I hope not. I would give a great deal to have a few minutes with our baby who died two days after birth. It hasn't happened. *Why not?*

The subject of divine intervention has occupied my thoughts a great deal the past ten years, and I've reached the conclusion that God doesn't grant miracles willy-nilly. Certainly not on demand. From personal experience I know it doesn't work to decide we are ready for a manifestation and announce that now is the time.

I am convinced miracles come to us as part of the greater plan, that they each accomplish a thing of worth in addition to offering comfort. For instance, Ida's husband returned to her not only to say good-by but also with an urgent message on temple work for a woman overlooked. Hack Severson was snatched from death by a stray bullet at the age of thirteen to complete a future of service important to the kingdom.

No, miracles don't come on demand. But I'm also convinced that they occur more often than we suppose, and that every family has at least one story they could tell. I submit that thought confidently because of all seventy-one chapters in all four of my books all but a handful have come from our intimate circle of family and friends. Granted our circle is wide, because we have traveled with my husband's employment. But my point is that proof of God's love and involvement in our lives is all around us.

The Lord is my shepherd. . . . He leadeth me beside the still waters. . . . Surely goodness and mercy shall follow me all the days of my life: and I will dwell in the house of the Lord for ever.